Pitching the Big Top:

How to Master the 3-Ring Circus of Federal Sales

Gene Moran
President
Capitol Integration

ISBN-13: Paperback 978-1-951407-04-9
ISBN-13: eBook 978-1-951407-05-6

Table of Contents

"…there are known unknowns; that is to say we know there are some things we do not know. But there are also unknown unknowns—the ones we don't know we don't know. And if one looks throughout the history of our country and other free countries, it is the latter category that tend to be the difficult ones." [1]

—Donald H. Rumsfeld, Former Secretary of Defense

[1] U.S. Department of Defense, Archives

PREFACE

This book is written for companies of any size striving to improve sales to the United States government. You'll learn my proven methodology to approach your government customer, organize your offering, position the funds for your contract and orchestrate your desired outcome—increased federal sales! You'll learn my method to better align with the government process, organize your pursuit with better purpose and truly know the status of the federal sale as the process unfolds. I have helped people like you and companies like yours achieve startling results. My framework of approaching federal sales is stunning in its simplicity, yet it has produced results for my clients measured in billions (with a B) of dollars.

While spending over one trillion dollars every year on discretionary[2] purchases, the US federal market remains among the largest markets in the world. Surprisingly, many companies selling to the US government rely on what is fundamentally a business-to-business sales strategy. Sadly, it's all too common. And it's wrong!

Companies selling to the US government are often out of alignment from the start. For example, such

---

[2]Think of discretionary purchases as variable expenses of government; they are decided upon and funded annually. Their corollaries are fixed purchases such as social security, Medicare and other entitlement programs. Those have been approved previously and must be funded annually; their elements are not re-competed annually.

companies identify and court an individual customer who is not the real buyer. It may also use customer resource management tools developed for commercial markets, which are ineffective in the government sales process. Additionally, decision-makers often have no real idea where the funds come from that fuel government contracts. This book reveals a much simpler way to view the process and yield better outcomes for both the government customer and your business.

I use the metaphor of the 3-ring circus to capture the concept of a highly complex process with many elements and distractions in motion at once. It all happens under the big top, yet some parts are interesting and meaningful while others are distractions or dead ends. Much like the performances of a 3-ring circus, the process of government sales never stops. Never. It remains in perpetual motion. Even when the government "shuts down."

I routinely directly help companies of all sizes to improve their positions and achieve significant improvements in federal sales outcomes. I have helped my clients master the 3-ring circus. This book will help you do the same.

Gene Moran
Washington, DC
October, 2019

Introduction—
The Big Picture

Why This Book?

Federal sales are hard. It's been made even more difficult over time by excessive oversight and review. Well-intended legislation, direction and policy derives from ever-recurring stories of "waste, fraud and abuse" in government. This book will save you time and money in your federal pursuits. You'll recognize where you may be wasting energy on the wrong part of the federal sales process. You'll gain confidence while recognizing how to know you are meeting with the right people at the right time. Most importantly, your federal sales prospects and results will begin to improve immediately.

When I studied political science in college, the rise of the military-industrial complex had been readily accepted in the government lexicon. Nearly 40 years later, the government sales process remains fundamentally unchanged. Guess what? The funding process that fuels sales is unlikely to change significantly in your professional lifetime.

I've been associated with some aspect of federal sales for more than 3 decades. I've seen and lived it from multiple perspectives: end user, decision maker, legislative liaison, corporate influencer and private practice in government relations. I've led trips and orchestrated meetings among people like Sen. John McCain, 4-star generals, members of Congress, Cabinet Members and Prime Ministers. I've been in the room where it happens.

My methodology for assessing and engaging the federal sales process is surprisingly easy. It underpins what I refer to as an engagement strategy. I'll specifically explain what I call the customer constellation: Your federal buyer isn't one person. Instead, it is a constellation of decision makers. Further, I'll outline the critical elements of timing and alignment. It works. It will work for you. If you don't master this concept, you'll continue to labor inefficiently while achieving suboptimal results.

While talking with company presidents, I am often surprised by their lack of working knowledge of the government funding process. That's because they think the rules of selling to the federal government are the same as selling to companies. That's an incorrect assumption. And that's why they fail to sell as much to the federal government as they could. They need a different playbook.

I work with companies with annual revenues from $5 million dollars to $15 billion dollars that want to expand their position in federal sales. My clients are company presidents, business unit vice presidents, business developers and sales team leaders. All wish to better command the full length and breadth of the government process.

The book is not a tutorial or how-to. It won't give you a magic checklist. It's bigger than that. As the title implies, it will identify three strategic rings of the federal funding and policy circus. They are rings of influence you might have ignored or of which you weren't fully aware. Knowing how to be the ringmaster will help you reach the success you desire.

Although I use a 3-ring circus as a metaphor for federal sales, I am not deriding or gibing the seriousness of our government mechanism. I find the imagery that a circus brings to mind to be relevant: one large spectacle, created through the orchestration of many moving parts to achieve an impressive result. One must appreciate the relative motion of numerous facets and players to understand how the whole picture comes together. The 3 rings are outlined in detail throughout the book. They are: *Industry, Agency and Congress.*

Pitching the Big Top: How to Master the 3-Ring Circus of Federal Sales reveals the larger process of how our government evaluates and adopts funding and policy decisions.

Through real-world and client examples, you'll see how companies like yours are succeeding beyond expectation. For reasons of company privacy, most brand names are removed, but the stories are real. You'll read examples and case studies of successful transactions I've conducted for my clients. Throughout, I hope to motivate you with questions designed to help improve your approach. You're likely to see you have been missing ways to close bigger federal sales. You might be surprised to find that you've lost out long before the acquisition began. I'll show you exactly how to overcome that problem.

You will learn how strategic alignment with the process early in the game will position you for a higher probability of the sale.

Within the 3 rings, you'll learn to navigate relationships and leverage information. You'll also learn the significance of the three years of opportunity that are always in front of you.

There are hundreds of books written on the subject of federal contracting. That's the problem: They tend to focus on the contract. This book takes you higher in the big tent. Observing the process from a bird's-eye view, you will see how to command all stages of the sales process—even long before the contract opportunity is announced.

You will build your own playbook for success as you progress through the examples, pro-tips and templates. You will see how to organize your government pursuits in a more efficient and thoughtful way. In doing so you'll step onto a faster path toward success in government sales.

It's All Relative

When I was a teenager, I raced offshore sailboats off the coast of South Florida. It was thrilling for a 4-person crew to guide a 30-to-40 foot boat around an ocean course, tight with competition and fraught with environmental challenges—wind, current, changing seas and afternoon thunderstorms. At the time, I didn't recognize the fundamental concept of relative motion—many things interacting at once on a desired outcome—winning! When I joined the Navy and began learning to drive ships, I soon recognized the same forces that affected sailboats also affected ships—albeit with greater consequence. From the time a ship takes in lines or weighs anchor, it is subject to relative motion. The road beneath a ship is always moving because of environmental conditions. Those must be considered and their effects evaluated and countered appropriately.

Flash forward to government sales in the 3-ring circus. Much like in sailboat racing and driving ships, I have assessed the concepts of relative motion are ever-present when pursuing an outcome with government. What am I talking about? You see, the many parts of the budget and policy process never stop moving, and they all move in relation to one another—relative motion. You need to appreciate this dynamic to get properly aligned to take part in the process. In the federal space you're entering a maelstrom. Success requires an appreciation and a mastery of the many moving parts.

About the Author

My name is Gene Moran. I spent a career as a US Navy Surface Warfare Officer, retiring as a Captain. I commanded the cruiser USS PHILIPPINE SEA, the destroyer USS LABOON and multi-ship operations in the Atlantic Ocean, Mediterranean Sea and Arabian Gulf. Ashore, I've worked at the Navy headquarters level advising Secretaries of the Navy, Chiefs of Naval Operations and Vice Chiefs of Naval Operations on legislative policy and budget negotiations with Congress. I've worked as a detailee, a senior Navy officer on loan to Congress, to the personal office of the Chairman of the Senate Appropriations Committee.

Additionally, I served in uniform as the Navy's principal liaison for the Senate and for appropriations matters in both the House and Senate. In those roles, I led dozens of Congressional delegations (CODELs) around the world, taking the most senior Senators and Representatives to meet with counterparts, Prime Ministers and international business leaders. I've spent time alone in unique settings with Members of Congress away from the fray. I appreciate how they think and understand what motivates them.

During my nearly 25 years in uniform, serving in 6 ships and more than 10 duty stations, visiting over 50 countries, I learned a few things about working within bureaucracies. I understand from personal experience the variations and exactness of rank structure, positional authority, informal authority, power, autonomy, strategy development, decision-making by a committee, decision-making by not deciding, deference to seniors, respect, accountability and federal funding.

That's a long and varied list, but those elements exist in every federal agency. I've learned to read the rooms, assess the situations, adjust the plans, pick up on subtleties, and apply the appropriate touches to influence desired sales outcomes. I want to share some of these experiences to help your business flourish in the federal space.

Upon leaving the US Navy, I recognized my skills transferred readily to the world of government relations (GR), the Washington, DC colloquialism for a federal salesperson. I became a corporate lobbyist for one of the largest defense companies in the United States, DRS Technologies, owned by one of the largest defense companies in the world, now Leonardo, SpA. As a Tier 2 supplier, I interacted with nearly every major prime in the US defense industry. Major primes are the really big defense companies such as General Dynamics, Lockheed Martin and Boeing. Tier 2 suppliers provide critical sub-systems and components to every major platform in the US inventory and in many more internationally. Major platforms are things like ships, tanks and airplanes. I represented dozens of defense programs to Congress and industry primes on behalf of DRS.

After several years as a Vice President and Senior Vice President of Corporate Government Relations, I gained an understanding of how the supply chains across all defense programs are fed, nurtured or ignored. I saw that countless company owners, executives and leaders, throughout the country, didn't understand the federal funding and policy process. They didn't know what they didn't know. I founded my own Government Relations firm, Capitol Integration, http://www.capitolintegration.com, so I could apply my skills and serve many companies in achieving their federal sales goals.

I'm a lobbyist. And you need to be one too! What am I talking about? In industry, salespeople who sell directly to the government are business developers. When presenting issues to Congress, that same GR person is suddenly a lobbyist. Lobbying is the same as sales. I educate decision makers to influence desired outcomes and get the government the best product or service. Sometimes, technology development outpaces the government's ability to know what it needs. I help with that, as well. In commercial sales, sales teams do the same thing—they educate and inform to make a sale.

I help clients achieve outsized results when selling to the federal government. Results can take the form of funding, favorable policy outcomes, or positive implementation of policy and contracts. I've developed a method that works for companies of all sizes attempting to close government business. My results measure to billions of dollars in favorable outcomes for clients. My clients range from large Fortune and NASDAQ-100 companies to 2-person startups that work out of a garage.

I've proven all companies have the same access to the federal funding and policy process. I've also learned many small and mid-size companies don't know how the federal acquisition process really works and how the government funds programs. I want to help you get better informed, better aligned and better integrated to get the best results possible in selling to the federal government. I want to help you sell your best product or policy idea to your best government customer.

I work directly with companies committed to strengthening their federal sales by solving government needs. The lessons of *Pitching the Big Top: How to Master the 3-Ring Circus of Federal Sales* are adaptable for corporate audiences in a keynote or seminar format. I can help your company see the 3 rings of the circus from a more strategic perspective.

If you are interested in working with my team at Capitol Integration, you can reach me directly at gene@capitolintegration.com.

My system works. It will work for you.
Let the show begin.

PART I:
Welcome to the Show

Chapter 1:
Circus Spectacle or
Organized Chaos?

"And so these men of Indostan
Disputed loud and long,
Each in his own opinion
Exceeding stiff and strong,
Though each was partly in the right,
And all were in the wrong!"

— Allegory of the 'Blind Men and the
Elephant'

Bill and Nancy Harris are scientists. They are a married couple that met working at a national laboratory. Both served full 20-year careers and earned a comfortable federal retirement. They are experts in polymer science. Bill and Nancy recognized the Department of Defense likely had many uses for polymers in their product requirements. They formed a small company, BN LLC, with the idea they could sell to the government.

It wasn't long before their Federal Business Opportunities (FBO), http://www.fbo.gov; alerts began to appear based on their tailored keyword searches. Bill and Nancy knew the government loads new business opportunities to the FBO website daily, opening up even playing field of potential vendors. BN LLC responded and won their first Small Business Innovation Research (SBIR) grant. The grant was for a Phase I SBIR in the amount of $125,000 to demonstrate a particular polymer application in clothing for soldiers. Bill and Nancy were thrilled.

As time went on, BN LLC responded to additional requests for proposals (RFPs). Each RFP seemed to be a perfect fit for BN LLC's core capability. They showed the utility of polymers in a variety of service applications to solve warfighter needs. But, after ten years of responding to RFPs and landing various levels of SBIR grants, BN LLC still did not have a solid connection to a specific, funded application in the field. They never rose above the experimentation level, merely dabbling in federal funding. It was a comfortable existence because they had already earned federal retirements, but Bill and Nancy hoped for more. They hoped the time would come that they'd be making sizeable profits while providing a meaningful warfighter solution.

That day never came.

Bill and Nancy didn't appreciate how agencies identify operational needs. Because they didn't understand the scope of the budget and policy process, they couldn't possibly get properly positioned to align with it—let alone get ahead of it. They were reacting to a public announcing system, FBO. They settled for near fits with various SBIRs and never understood how the decision-making process for federal funding really works. They couldn't convert their SBIR victories into funded programs of record status. Effectively, BN LLC operated at a steady plateau for its entire existence. Bill and Nancy were often ill informed, out of alignment and far behind in the process. As a result, the ground they operated on inevitably eroded.

In Washington, DC, if it's not funded, it's not real.

Now, let's turn it back to you. The reason you may have missed out on a government contract this fiscal year or didn't secure your desired level of funding is not because you have an inferior product or idea. You are undoubtedly an expert in your field, and you probably are working just as hard as your competitors. The difference between earning a contract and being left by the wayside isn't working harder—*it's working smart*.

To leverage the maximum outcome from the federal sales process you must actively take part in a much fuller funding and policy process that begins long before the contract opportunity ever develops. You must also appreciate the myriad ways in which buying decisions and policy decisions are identified, influenced, evaluated, and funded.

Most companies sell their products or services at the wrong end of the acquisition and contracting process. It's easy to fall into this trap. From the entrepreneurial startup, to the "gold standard" Big Primes of the US defense market, inexperience and bad information are rampant. Few people fully understand the orbit of events and players that surround the creation of a government contract. If you have found yourself left out of federal business opportunities, you are not alone.

Test Yourself: Check the boxes that apply to you:

☐ You believe you have a superior product or service.

☐ You want a federal contract.

☐ You can't find the "right" buyer.

☐ Your product "just missed the cut line" this year.

☐ Your funding was "reprogrammed."

☐ You were told your project was in the budget.

☐ You were told my project would be in next year's budget (calendar year or fiscal year…do you know?)

☐ You attend industry trade shows to network.

☐ You "invest" in trade show booth space.

☐ Your competition gets interviewed on professional panels at conferences.

☐ You read about competitor's products in trade magazines.

☐ You get directed to the Small Business Liaison Office.

☐ You get small SBIR contracts but are not able to advance them to maturity.

☐ You get promised a "sweep up funds" that never materializes.

If you checked one or more of these boxes, you have come to the right place. You will learn the right process to get funded.

The Process

Within federal acquisitions, there are essentially two tracks that run in tandem with one another to create the broader process—funding and policy.

Let's start with funding.

Figure 1: The Funding Process Timeline

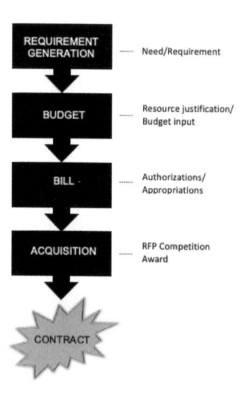

Selling to the government is a long and never-ending process. The basic phases are depicted in Figure 1. Many people make the mistake of starting at the acquisition phase when the sales process actually begins much earlier. Ideally, starting at the requirement generation phase makes the most sense. You'll see there are times when you can enter at the budget or bill phase, and we'll discuss that later in this book.

It's easy to fall into the trap of focusing on the acquisition phase—or starting at the end. After all, at the acquisition end of the spectrum it's pretty clear that funding is, or will soon be, available. It's fairly simple to track the status of a contract notification and competition process. FBO serves as the most transparent way for government agencies to share relevant information with all interested parties simultaneously, thereby avoiding the appearance of favor. At that late stage, funding has generally fallen into place and the agency knows it can actually afford what it hopes to buy using that specific contract.

However, throughout the 3-ring circus I'll point out numerous places where an effective sales team can influence the end-game long before the contracting process begins. Making the effort to apply your team's best efforts at an earlier point on the process can dramatically increase your probability of win. These 3 rings will be introduced in more detail shortly, but you can see a foreshadowing of their significance to the process. Industry, agency and Congress each have prominent roles at different points along the funding spectrum. Understanding the 3-ring circus will help you know the left and middle portions of the funding spectrum long before the contract win at the end.

If you've waited until the contract stage to throw your hat in the ring, it's already too late.

Let's move on to the policy process.

Policy formulation has a timeline similar to the funding timeline in Figure 1, along which most companies can align and influence. Agencies have numerous inherent authorities derived over time, and in many cases, derived over years of policies overlaying one another. Standardized practices and procedures evolve over time and are the rules by which the agency executes its mission.

Figure 2. Policy Process Timeline

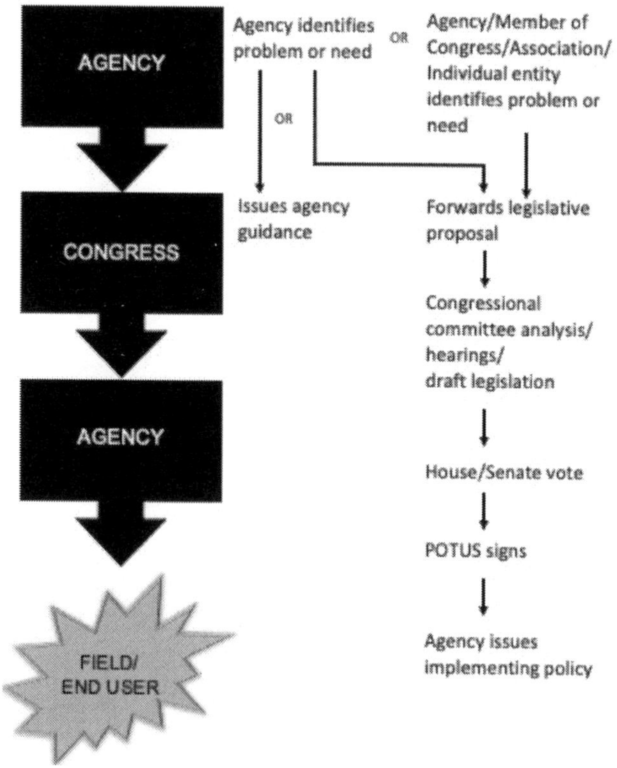

For our purposes, let's consider two types of policy: agency policy and implementing policy, stemming from a specific piece of legislation. The point at which a policy idea is introduced determines whether or not it is agency policy or implementing policy. Figure 2 indicates that an agency can set policy stemming from its inherent authorities. A situation requiring a position or standardization by the agency is put in place, usually via an appropriate directive, by agency leadership.

When I speak of implementing policy, I'm referring to policy meant to put a piece of legislation into action. Implementing policy can originate from any number of inputs to the process. The key here is that Congress took its vote and legislated some part of the policy outcome. The implementing policy is the agency's instruction for how to operationalize the legislative direction.

Example:

Our federal trade policy strives to protect the US defense industrial base. For decades, across multiple administrations, the US has seen the political benefit of having a trade policy that favors US business. In this case, trade policy has a political connotation. Through the annual National Defense Authorization Act (NDAA), Congress legislates specifics of how US trade policy should favor US businesses in defense acquisitions—"Buy America" is a broad moniker for such legislation. DoD implements legislation via agency directives as agency policy. The Defense Acquisition Regulation Supplement (DFARS) is an agency-wide directive implementing policy.[3]

It's one thing to not comply with a policy. It's quite another thing to not comply with the law.

Welcome to the Circus

Figure 3: The 3 Rings of the Federal Sale

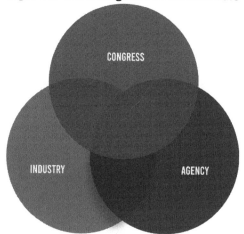

---

[3]You'll note that this book will often rely on examples from the defense industry but the broader lessons in this and subsequent chapters can apply to any industry or business area engaging with the federal government. The US defense budget is the largest segment of the annual discretionary budget by a factor of ten. In fiscal year 2020, the US defense budget exceeds $725 billion.

The 3 rings represent three areas of influence that open the door to dozens of opportunities to influence the process well before the contract phase.

As you can now see, the policy process and funding process are both parallel and woven together through our government structure. Whether you are hoping to impact one, the other or both, it is imperative that you appreciate all the forces swirling around you so you can engage in a synchronized manner.

Throughout Part I, I'll review each of the 3 rings of influence to help you better appreciate their elements and determine how their relative positioning allows you to achieve *maximum influence to produce outsized outcomes in funding and policy support.*

Chapter 2: The Animal Acts– Every Circus Has Them

"Start where you stand, and work with whatever tools you may have at your command, and better tools will be found as you go along."
—Napoleon Hill, American Author

I worked with a medium-sized company ($50 million in revenue) that specializes in manufacturing highly sensitive components used in high-end classified defense programs. The company is an internationally recognized industry leader. As international trade disputes with China began to increase in 2018 and 2019, conflicting laws and policies began to put extraordinary pressure on the supply chain for its components. Some components relied on rare earth material only available in China. The United States government had allowed its US industrial base of rare earth material to shrink to a critical low point, yet was pressuring China by forbidding US suppliers from using these foreign materials in US weapons systems.

I was brought in to help the company improve its position. Together we mapped an engagement plan for interacting with agencies within DoD and with Congress.

Over time, decision-makers in the Office of the Secretary of Defense (OSD) and Congress came to understand that policies and laws were in conflict with each other and were preventing good government solutions. We successfully educated them so that logical work-arounds and exceptions were written into policy updates and relevant legislation. In this case, the client knew the industry ring of influence quite well. Imagine that: a company of this size can actually influence foreign policy decisions.

Figure 4: The Industry Ring

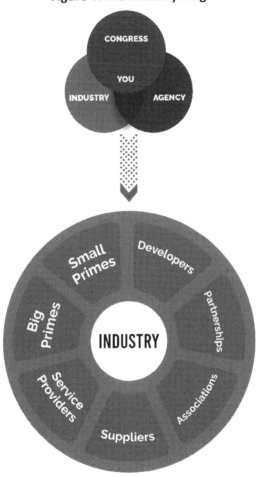

Going it alone can be a dangerous and unprofita-ble strategy. Your success rate will be much higher if you find allies you can work with. It's easy to miss the many opportunities to grow relationships. We're often so busy executing our own business plan we miss out on the benefits of working with a partner on at least part of the desired outcome together.

- **Big primes** are the largest companies and typically provide significant influence within the segments of the industries in which they participate.

- **Small primes** serve critical roles, but don't pack as big of a punch with industry trends or influence presence in DC. They are often "subs" to the big primes.

- **Developers** bring new technologies and solutions into the industry ecosphere.

- **Suppliers** provide components or other elements necessary for solutions.

- **Service providers** operate at every level of the industry (like lawyers and accountants).

- **Partnerships** (formal and informal) exist between companies within the industry at different levels, such as joint ventures and teams.

- A myriad of **associations** exist within most industries representing its various sub-segments. At the Washington, DC level, there

> are thousands of associations that exist to
> oversee and influence collective interests.

Some players operate across multiple industries. You might find members of your primary industry community thriving in other industry communities. Think of large companies such as General Electric (aviation, rail, healthcare, appliances and lighting), Amazon (where isn't Amazon?), and NXP (automotive, secure ID, mobile communications). Observing this domain, it is likely you can identify where your business, and your competition, fit within your industry ring.

Does the Big Prime Always Know More?

Primes often exert outsized influence within the industry community. The reason is simple: they have the resources to be in many places at one time and participate across the full spectrum of industry activities. The tremendous influence enjoyed by the big primes can become problematic when they are your industry customers or partners. You may find yourself in this scenario: you are selling to a prime, and because they are the "big dog," in the industry you follow their directions and do everything in your power to maintain a positive and mutually respectful relationship. Sound familiar?

Here's the problem:
Bigger doesn't always translate to better informed.

Primes often speak for the industry, but they might not always be the best source of information. It is critical for you to know where your direct contact at the prime company is getting their industry knowledge, information and day-to-day intelligence. The first thing to recognize is at what level are you connected to the prime?

- Procurement buyer? The individual who can issue a purchase order.

- Program management? The individual charged with executing the program to a specific cost and time schedule.

- Profit and Loss (P&L) leadership? The individuals accountable for meeting the prescribed profit margins that determine the cost and time schedules.

- Executive team? The company leaders who decide what technologies and solutions on which the company will stake its future.

In the simplest terms, as relates to the caliber of your prime contacts, you could read this list from top to bottom as Good, Better, Best, and Solid Gold. The quality of information you receive from your contacts is likely inversely proportional to their position on this list. The more junior the connection, the less likely that individual is "plugged in" to the big picture.

Let's Test This

Say the big prime puts out a request for proposal (RFP) soliciting inputs on your part of a future federal purchase. They tell you the government plans to build fourteen widgets. You see an opportunity and take it at face value. You diligently prepare and submit a proposal. You insert the opportunity into your funnel and assign it a probability of "win." Then, you wait, but the bid doesn't get awarded. You learn from your prime contact that the agency delayed the purchase of widgets for unspecified reasons.

Poof, your financial plan now has a hole. No way can you make your number this late in the year. You became a victim of bad information. Worse, the mis-interpretation introduced a risk to your company, and *maybe to you personally*. This might seem like an extreme example, but it happens regularly.

The lesson here is that you have the power to know as much as the big prime. I'll outline more in subsequent chapters about exactly how. Your go-to contact at the prime could be your greatest, most well-informed ally or, worst ill-informed enemy. It is possible that what they relay to you is a wholesale acceptance of whatever explanations the organizational leadership gave them. Or, maybe what they tell you is what their poorly informed federal customer told them. Many subs accept the word of the prime as infallible. In reality, suppliers often decide based on poor or incomplete information that you may be able to access. Don't be a victim. There is no reason you cannot be better informed about the status of your program than the prime or the federal customer. You should have the tools to know at least as much as they do about the expected trajectory of a program. You can know if the policy and funding are in place, will imminently be in place, or are far from being in place.

Big primes will act in their best interest. They must. As publicly traded companies they have a responsibility to their shareholders. Be mindful that their best interests may not always align with your best interests. Be informed.

I will show you how to find, use and exploit the required tools when we discuss the customer network in Chapter 5. But first, let's fill out the rest of the industry ring.

Service Providers

Service providers are critical to any industry. All businesses have common needs for functional external support. These can include legal counsel, human resources, accounting and proposal writing. Most companies rely on various forms of service provider support from external vendors. It makes good business sense to outsource some of these specialty areas.

Service providers serve competitors, operating with a non-disclosure agreement (NDA) in place. While the intention of NDAs is to provide restrictions on the mutual exchange of proprietary information, they don't keep your service provider from sharing useful bits of market intelligence. Business developers often view the signature of an NDA as a critical step in the customer qualification process and spend little time on the details of the actual agreement. Take the time to understand the limitations *and the level of flexibility* that NDAs can allow. Service providers are always in the industry swim, attending trade shows, seminars, events and panels. Their business relies on developing new clients every year. As a result, many of your service providers are likely participating in far more professional events than you can attend.

Use their market intelligence. Engage them on the broader industry, beyond your ongoing service needs. This may provide invaluable information that can help you make the sale.

Sounds simple; few take full advantage.

For Your Playbook:

Ask your accountant, attorney or human resources manager about their upcoming trade show attendance plans. See where that thread takes you.

Partners

Partners can take several forms. Common forms of partnership include Joint Ventures (JVs) and Teaming Agreements (TAs). JVs and TAs differ from the more traditional prime to small prime relationships in that the participants view themselves more as equals. While not always a 50-50 relationship, they're in the pursuit together and each provides a unique value to the relationship. It's not that the prime doesn't recognize the small prime's value, but the prime is definitely the boss and lead decision maker in those relationships. Partnering can be a way to extend your breadth, allowing you to participate more fully, exert more influence within your industry and grow your company faster. Smaller companies often resist the concept of partnerships for fear of giving up control. Keeping an open mind for strategic opportunities to join forces opens the potential to speed up your business by orders of magnitude. Every major prime is interested in partnering at some level. Shared burden is always welcome. Your business may qualify for special set-asides designated for companies of a specific qualified category: small business, woman-owned or veteran-owned. Partnering with the larger company qualifies them for your special category. You can help each other by working together. It's an exceptionally common occurrence—*you don't have to go it alone*. Be mindful, when big primes become your sub in order to qualify for your special category, they are used to being big primes, not subs. You may be challenged when trying to direct larger companies. It will boil down to style and personality, but corporate cultures are a reality you'll be forced to deal with.

For Your Playbook:

- *List three companies with which you could reasonably partner to pursue a larger opportunity.*

- *Identify three potential obstacles to those partnerships and how you might overcome them.*

- *Ask yourself, "Am I willing to share the challenges with a partner in pursuit of a larger outcome?"*

Associations

Now, let's focus on the role of associations within your industry. Associations serve multiple purposes, which include:

1. Representing common policy interests of its members.

2. Assisting with establishing industry standards (sometimes offering certification programs).

3. Providing platforms for an open exchange of ideas: trade shows, seminars, panels, and networking receptions.

4. Offering communications and media messaging within the industry.

Thousands of associations have a presence in Washington, DC. There's a reason for that. Voices of influence are louder and better understood when they are heard at the point of maximum impact— where the government makes funding and policy decisions. Whether it's a group of 100, 1,000 or 10,000, multiple voices speaking as one resonate with amplified influence.

Example:

Why do AARP memberships arrive in the mail on your 50th birthday— over a decade before traditional retirement age? AARP recognized long ago that the strength of numbers is a significant advantage in the influence business. Therefore, they engage in a mail campaign to allow members to sign up well before coming of retirement age.

Do you know the associations that exist to represent interests that matter to your business? Are you a member? Should you be a leader? You may think you don't have time for such extras given the demands on your plate, but let's pick that apart a bit.

It's relevant to know the structures of the boards of directors and governance committees at the different associations within your industry. Many associations have committees and subcommittees that serve the dual purpose of dividing the work, while assuring avenues of input from the membership. Typically, associations have a volunteer board of directors, typically associated with a qualifying membership fee. A qualifying fee? Yes, companies pay for these seats, and you can too! Payment might take the form of a straight annual fee, sponsorship, underwriting or exchange of services. Sometimes, board seats carry multiple votes, again associated with a qualifying membership fee. Other boards have by-laws that align their seats according to other elements of the membership besides associated fees. Revenue, headcount and customer base are common sub-categories of association membership. The idea is to assure some degree of representation across the membership. Understanding the association structures relevant to your business opens the door for you to take a meaningful and visible role within your industry.

Participating in association leadership can be a useful business development technique and help further distinguish your voice.

Example:

When I was a corporate lobbyist, and later a private consultant, I was a volunteer board member with the Florida Defense Contractors Association (FDCA). FDCA is a statewide organization that brings defense primes and suppliers together to advance their common interests in the defense industry of Florida. As a by-product of volunteering I gained exposure to, and observed conversations between, countless industry influencers throughout the state.

As a result of this experience, I was able to connect companies, potential primes, partners and suppliers so they could have an inside track toward future government sales.

Because of the many audiences with which associations communicate, you will find helpful angles that may further a business position or gain an audience with decision makers who might otherwise be out of your reach.

Associations are great business development tools.

Many agency acquisition decision makers such as Program Executive Officers (PEOs), Program Managers (PMs) and Contracting Officers (KOs—not a typo; only the government would abbreviate like this) only conduct their communication with an industry via associations. This communications channel is advantageous because it allows government figures to avoid the perception of unfair access, which may arise if they were only to schedule individual meetings with certain industry members in their government office. Going through an association maintains an appearance of inclusivity.

Tapping into the channel of an association is a perfect opportunity for you to connect with your government customer and make your voice heard.

There is no shortage of associations — participating wisely is good for business.

For Your Playbook:

List three associations with which you could reasonably partner to pursue a larger opportunity.

Putting it into Practice — The Engagement Strategy

Once you have identified the relevant individuals in your industry ring, you must incorporate them into your selling strategy. You'll then want to capture them in an engagement plan that is practical, legible and efficient for you and your business partners.

Figure 5 depicts the beginning of an engagement plan template I will build upon throughout the book. It can serve as a visual representation of a selling strategy incorporating the Industry, Agency and Congress

rings of influence. Industry is the first building block of this plan. As I introduce new concepts throughout the book, I will add and populate the cells. For a template of an engagement plan matrix we use at Capitol Integration, go to
http://www.capitolintegration.com/3-ringcircus.

Figure 5: The Engagement Plan – Part I

ISSUE A (FY 3)	Title			Message	Notes	Contact
Industry						
Bill Jones	VP, Supply Chain			We need to notify suppliers of 3-year forecast	Speaking at Industry Day	Bjones@prime.com
Terry Smith	Contracting officer			We must be on contract by 1 May.		

Chapter 3: The High Wire— Aerial Artists of Bureaucracies

"The most terrifying words in the English language: I'm from the government and I'm here to help."

—*Ronald Reagan*

A large multi-national NASDAQ-100 Company wanted to extend its highly successful product offering from the Department of Defense into adjacent markets in the Department of Veteran's Affairs (VA) and Department of Health and Human Services (HHS). They knew their way around their primary customer agency in DoD, but recognized the potential for exploring other government agencies.

The company brought me in to specifically open doors, educate agency officials and identify contract opportunities. I assisted with mapping decision-makers in VA and HHS, focusing on the most appropriate entry points that allowed an efficient and cost-effective method of pursuit.

After engaging with the VA and HHS, the company made the strategic decision to not pursue these particular opportunities. When they better understood those markets, they didn't see the same potential. Sometimes going through the process of learning and identifying agency decision-makers helps you make a sound decision not to proceed. In this case, they made a decision to avoid a costly pursuit.

Core Functions of Agencies

Regardless of the department in which they reside, agencies have several core functions in common. Agencies specifically:

- Identify and assess needs in the field.

- Validate needs as requirements.

- Allocate resources to acquire solutions.

Success in garnering favorable funding and policy outcomes in any federal agency requires an appreciation of these core functions.

Agencies Begin With People

There are dozens of agencies within the federal government. The organizational structures amongst these various agencies are similar, although not identical. Regardless of the variations in positions, titles, uniforms, geographic locations and headquarters personnel, what truly make each agency unique are the people. The people who perform the functions of government come from all walks of life, with different motivations and ambitions. For example, some may be content to have a steady job; some aspire to lead a department or agency. Understanding the very human dynamics at play can help you better relate to the people with whom you'll interact and the manner in which they approach their work. Making the effort to understand the mechanics of the organization to which you are selling will make a huge difference.

Now, let's take a closer look at the agency ring of influence.

Bureaucrat—Friend or Foe?

The agency ring refers to the government agency to which you hope to sell. There are dozens of agencies across multiple departments of government. While it may appear that some agencies are relatively opaque to the outsider, they are penetrable. You just have to figure out the right contact and offer a compelling reason for making the connection. Read on.

Figure 6: The Agency Ring

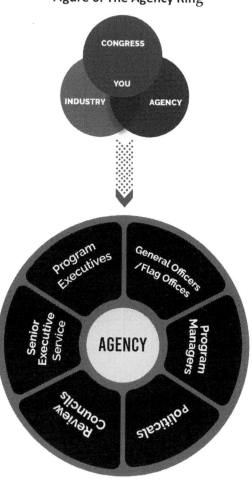

Let me dispel a few myths and misconceptions about government bureaucrats. By definition, they are duty-bound to abide by the countless rules, constraints on their authority and compliance with layer upon layer of oversight demands. It's not their fault that, over time, many government employees gravitate toward a "don't rock the boat" manner of executing their duties. The layers of protection meant to keep the agency from running amok take the form of committees, review authorities and highly concentrated decision-making. These layers would wear on anyone.

The overarching goal is good government; balancing pursuit of best while remaining mindful of taxpayer cost.

Publicly traded companies have a fiduciary responsibility to their shareholders first, then to their customers.

Government agencies have a responsibility to the ideals of the Constitution and the taxpayers who fund government pursuits.

This might be a broad generalization, but most government agency employees are proud to serve their country, supporting something bigger than them. Money is not the motivation for most people; it is a matter of service.

To be clear, this doesn't excuse poor performance. But, it is important to invoke a better level of understanding when working within a government agency that you may not have considered. The better you appreciate the working conditions of your agency counterparts, the easier it will be to establish and forge meaningful business relationships. When you interact with people, try to relate to them. Without prying or being obsequious, you can gently ask how they're doing? How's morale? Relate an item in the news to their organization or position. I'm often amazed at how readily people will open up with a few unexpected words. The key is not to press. Ask a few friendly questions and let them talk. If they don't bite, that's okay. It comes with time. The mistake many salespeople make is failing to read the room and continuing to press. I'll share in much greater detail how to prepare your message for a meeting in Part II. For now, remember they are people just like you. They have families, interests, frustrations and goals. Lend an ear.

The Organization Chart

Government agencies fall into four categories: cabinet departments, independent executive agencies, independent regulatory agencies and government corporations. Organization charts define the formal order. Position descriptions (PDs) define all funded positions within government organization charts. All PDs go through a highly formalized review process that spells out all specific duties and responsibilities in extraordinary detail. We'll talk more in Chapter 5 about the differences of formal positional authorities versus informal authority, influence and power.

The four agency bureaucracies differ in scope and breadth of authorities as well as in the way they make position appointments. For our purposes, these differences are not relevant. The tips and tricks associated with connecting with an agency apply across the board.

At the top of an agency organization chart are the Cabinet-level Secretaries or an equivalent Administrator or Director. They are political appointees. Colloquially, agencies call these individuals "politicals." Immediately below the political level are various levels of civil servants. The most senior civilians comprise the Senior Executive Service (SES)—they are senior career officials. Within uniformed services such as DoD, USCG, US Public Health Service and NOAA, SES counterparts are called General Officers or Flag Officers (GOFOs). Next come senior civilian positions of varying grades and steps from the most junior GS-1 to the more senior GS-15. Congress must authorize and fund all federal positions. Because of this, formal changes to an organization chart are deliberate and relatively uncommon.

Figure 7: Excerpt of the DoD Organization Chart[4]

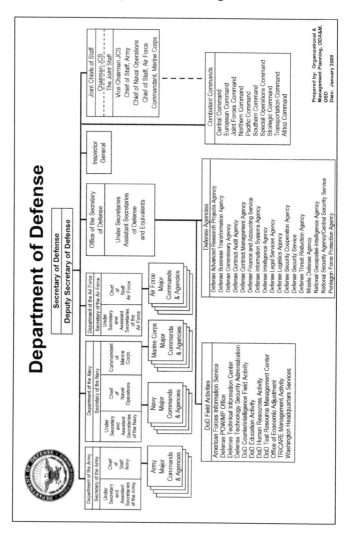

[4] http://www.netage.com/economics/gov/images-org/DoD-org-chart.pdf

Seniority is one thing; functional organizational control is another. Politicals—the Cabinet Secretaries, Under Secretaries, Assistant Secretaries, Principal Deputy Assistant Secretaries—all implement administration policies. In theory, those policies represent strategic directions stemming from a President's agenda. The agenda is implemented via both policy directives and funding. I said it earlier and will probably repeat it many times: if it's not funded, it's not real. The various bureaucracies amongst government agencies carry out the policy and funding decisions made in Congress.

Resourcing Versus Acquisitions: Two Ends of the Process

Recall the funding process timeline in Figure 8. There are two ends with very different purposes:

Figure 8: The Funding Process Timeline

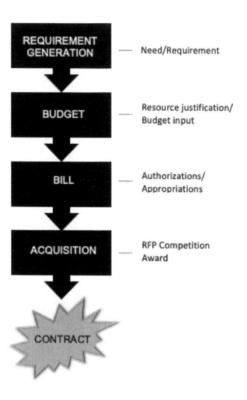

Resource sponsors are agency officials charged with evaluating needs identified in the field. They oversee requirements generation and approval. When you hear resourcing, think funding. They are synonymous terms. Resource sponsors determine what they can fund against the backdrop of funding constraints, strategic objectives and the agenda of the administration. They *test the operational needs, validate the need and generate a requirement*. A requirement is a documented validation of need. It may sometimes be referred to in the context of a requirements document. Without a requirement, the acquisition process doesn't proceed. There can be many unmet needs within an agency; if resource sponsors don't validate needs as requirements, the agency alone won't fund them.

Remember this sequence: needs, requirements and resources (these are the inputs).

Example:

Clever US Customs and Border Protection agents recognized that surveillance of US borders by traditional manned methods (vehicles, planes and observation posts) was not enough. They saw that aerial surveillance and technology could extend their range of border coverage.

They defined an operational need: They could not keep up using existing surveillance methods. The sector-level agents couldn't just go out and buy an aerostat or small unmanned aerial vehicle. Nor could they buy the sophisticated communications gear to connect these aerial resources with a command-and-control system. This need generated a new requirement. The agency then requested that requirement be included in the President's budget request to Congress. The program ultimately grew into the Secure Border Initiative (SBI).

The need became an input to the larger process.

Pro-tip:

*This early phase of the decision process might be the
best time to lay the groundwork for your product
or service. Knowing who makes these early capability decisions can provide you with an advantage.*

SES and GOFO-level officials typically lead resource sponsors and are staffed with subordinates of
commensurate rank and authorities. There are numerous methods by which resource sponsors evaluate and determine funding for capabilities. DoD uses
multiple committees and panels composed of service-
specific, joint, or multi-agency stakeholders. While
the resource sponsor determines which capabilities to
purchase, it's the acquisition world that takes the
steps to buy the product or service. Program executives, acquisition officials, contracting officials and
warrant holders all comprise elements of the acquisition apparatus within a federal agency. The specific
titles vary by the agency, but the functions are the
same.

Collectively, the acquisition officials seek to find
the best solution (a sometimes subjective term) for the
defined requirement. These agents are responsible for
acquiring or purchasing the products, technology and
services they need to function as an agency. Their
functions reside at the far right of Figure 8.

Acquisition officials deal with delivering outputs (products/services).

Some program officials are civilians who do not rotate frequently, while others are field personnel who cycle fairly regularly in and out of headquarters level assignments. Within most program offices you will see functional leads such as heads of legal and financial. There will also be some version of a small business office (SBO) or other external relations arm. Last, there will be a Program Manager or Deputy Program Manager. This is the person you may believe to be (and treat as) your actual customer—unfortunately; it's not that simple. These positions within your relevant agency are essential, but not the only, points of contact on the web that stretches across your industry, agency and Congress rings. I'll delve deeper into this idea in Chapter 5, and will present options that can help you speed up this process for your product, service or idea.

Putting it into Practice—The Engagement Strategy

Figure 9 depicts agency contacts added to the engagement strategy. We want to keep track of the officials associated with decisions affecting our issue or funding. Notice, we now have two of the three rings of influence with their own section of the engagement strategy. For a template of an engagement plan matrix we use at Capitol Integration, go to www.capitolintegration/3-ringcircus.

Figure 9: The Engagement Plan – Part II

ISSUE A (FY 3)	Title				Message	Notes	Contact
Industry							
Bill Jones	VP, Supply Chain				We need to notify suppliers of 3-year forecast	Speaking at Industry Day	Bjones@prime.com
Terry Smith	Contracting officer				We must be on contract by 1 May		
Agency							
Mr. Big	Asst Secretary				Foreign competition is a concern.		jking@agency.gov
Mike Richards	Program Mgr				RFP must be issued by 31 Jan		mrichards@agency.gov
Ms. King	Scheduler/EA					Don't call on Mondays	jking@agency.gov

Chapter 4: The Contortionists—Who Makes Congress Work

"All politics is local."
—Tip O'Neill

An employee-owned company successfully provided engineering products to US Navy ships for over 50 years. In recent years, technology advances allowed for a significant improvement over the widely-accepted and installed systems. But the company leadership couldn't get the US Navy to recognize the lifecycle savings to be achieved after an initial additional investment was made. The newer technology was safer for sailors to operate and cheaper when measured over the life of the ship, but there was no incentive for the short-term cost increase to install this improvement.

After several years of trying to convince the Navy, they came to me. I helped the company tell their story more effectively to more stakeholders in their customer constellation. Congressional committees agreed that conducting a pilot project could be a low-risk way to slowly introduce the improved capability in specific ship types. Congress funded the pilot project as an increase to the President's Budget request.

Aboard an US Army HH-60 Blackhawk en route to the Kuwait Airport:

We were completing another visit to the war zone where Senator John McCain's Congressional delegation (CODEL) had received the latest updates from leaders on the ground in Iraq: General Petraeus, Ambassador Crocker and Saudi Prime Minister Al-Maliki.

As was typical, we had flown overnight via Gulfstream military jet from Joint Base Andrews on a Thursday night, arriving in Kuwait Friday morning. A waiting C-130 Hercules transport, the workhorse of intra-theater lift and transport, would launch as fast as we boarded and our minimal hand luggage could be secured in place.

Spending Friday and Saturday at multiple locations in Iraq was the norm for these trips. Meals with troops, meetings with leaders, transits between headquarters, detailed briefings from staffs and diplomatic courtesies with Iraqi leaders. The days were intensely long and without breaks.

Senator McCain had literally held my job as Director of the Navy Senate Liaison office when he was a Navy Captain decades earlier. He knew what it took to make these trips run smoothly and trusted his foreign policy aide and me to run appropriate interference to do just that.

We were returning via Kuwait to catch our waiting Gulfstream military jet home. Five passengers (3 senators, 1 aide and me) were together in the final hel-icopter ride before meeting the jet. We were ready for a quick shower at the base before getting on the jet. We were tight on time and on the verge of running late. Flying into headwinds east always made the ride back to the US longer. Due to the helicopter noise, I wrote on an index card and showed it to Sen. McCain: "We have a meal waiting on the flight back. Shower? Yes or no?" Without hesitation or a vote from the others, he pointed to "No."

I could see the shoulders of the group slump. We were pressing on to make the 10-hour flight back home rather than take 20 minutes to clean up. I could feel the others asking themselves, "Why the hell did you even ask him that question?" It was a fair question for them to feel, but it was also CODEL McCain. We would be jumping straight from the helicopter to the jet.

This shower decision was a typical McCain call as I had observed during several such trips with him. Being late wasn't a good thing. Driven. No time to waste. Let's go. It was always a front row seat on history in the making.

We did have the compulsory BSF (Brief Stop for Fuel) at Shannon, Ireland. Shannon Airport takes pride in its efficient service and its quaint Irish pub where one could have a quick pint of Guinness while the plane refueled...but no time for a shower. By Monday CODEL travelers would be back to their Washington, DC schedules.

As with most CODELs where I took other Members of Congress on their fact-finding or diplomatic missions, I can attest the workdays of the Members are long. Their advance preparation and study is always on display and time is always the non-renewable resource. Senator McCain and his leadership of such trips set the bar for covering a lot of ground in minimal time.

Appreciating the significance of time in Congressional work, and throughout the federal process, can change how you approach decision makers. I'll teach you how to maximize your moment when it comes.

My Inside View of High-Level Congressional Engagement

I regularly accompanied the Secretary of the Navy and Chief of Naval Operations to meet with senior Members of Congress, Chairmen of House and Senate Armed Services Committees and Chairmen of House and Senate Appropriations Committees. Most meetings took place in Capitol Hill offices, but occasionally they were in the Pentagon.

Most senior agency leaders have similar meeting schedules with members of Congress. It's critical that such dialogue be of a recurring nature for the mutual benefit of government. Staff tries mightily to keep the meetings. The beauty of the small group meetings among leaders from all three rings of influence is that real ideas and solutions are exchanged—outside the media spotlight. Constraints on decisions become better understood. It's not the smoky back room some imagine. It's professionals exchanging views and attempting to reconcile conflicting demands and expectations.

As a result, I learned success in dealing with government officials absolutely requires you to get outside of your own bubble and try to put yourself in the other's shoes. If you deal honestly with people, you'll be pleasantly surprised at what can be accomplished. If you are perceived to be working a personal agenda or a lopsided outcome, you'll get what you deserve.

Figure 10: The Congress Ring

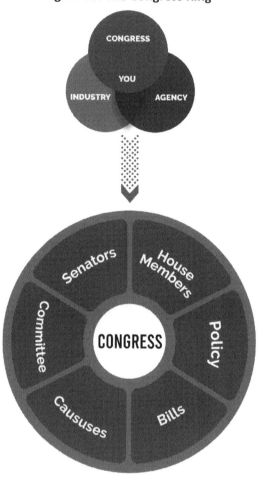

To this point, you might not have thought much about the role Congress plays in your business. You still might not think their decisions have much impact. Let's just pause for a minute and dismiss that notion:

If you are selling to the Federal Government, Congress funds and oversees policies that affect every aspect of your business.

The Budget Makers

The role of Congress in the acquisition process is to establish policies and pass legislation that authorizes and appropriates funds for *all* federal spending. In theory, before spending legislation moves forward, Congress should agree on an overall topline budget. The congressional budget is a Concurrent Resolution, an agreement between the House and Senate leadership on how they will allocate funding and divide it across the government. The congressional budget is not a law; the President does not sign it.

You will hear in the media many references to "the congressional budget," "the President's budget," or amounts that have been "authorized," versus amounts that have been "appropriated." These terms all reference completely different things. It is no wonder that executives, business owners and industry practitioners routinely mix up the terms. I'll highlight the various distinctions to make you an informed participant in the federal process. However, know that most others in your industry, and the media, may not be so precise.

When people talk about "the budget" without clarifying which one they mean, it spells confusion. If you hear someone casually tossing around references to "the budget," help that person be more precise and ask, which one? If you see that 'x' amount of money will fund a certain program or agency, ask them if that amount that was authorized or appropriated? It matters—be knowledgeable and be careful (Chapter 7 goes into this topic in further detail).

Key Terms:

President's Budget (PB)—A consolidated input to Congress outlining priorities and requesting funding.

Congressional Budget—An agreement in Congress; not signed into law.

Authorization—Legislation that authorizes policies and funding.

Appropriation—Legislation that approves the allocation of funds.

The Legislators

Congress also legislates policy. The topics addressed by Congress are varied and vast. Moreover, as the political winds shift over time, Congressional policy on these myriad subjects will inevitably change. Within this political vortex, and in an era of sound bites, it has become very easy for old information to take on an extended life, with mythical staying power.

Pro Tip:

Assuring that Congress is working with the most updated facts and figures to make informed policy decisions is paramount. Offering this information to them as an industry expert is your opportunity to maintain an ongoing dialogue. Take advantage.

Members of Congress and their staffs have a lot of different issues on their plates. They can easily fall behind on the most current information about your issue.

Example:

The Littoral Combat Ship (LCS) became an industry symbol of a poorly conceived program rushed into production before the design was mature. Well-intended efforts to speed up the acquisition system with less rigid adherence to design standards ultimately proved costly in both dollars and time. The development of mission modules was a disaster. As a result, the first ships off the line lacked standardization and were subject to costly rework. Congress heaped the blame for these costly missteps on the Navy and industry.

To salvage the program, industry took the lead in helping the Navy find a new way forward. Ship quality improved dramatically in very measurable ways, although mission module progress still lagged. Industry ship manufacturers made sure Congress and the Navy could see the distinction and identify more precisely where the program would benefit from additional corrective action.

Had industry not engaged so directly with Congress, it is likely the early negative headlines would have led to program cancellation, the loss of thousands of jobs and at least one shipyard closing. Industry shaped a dramatically different outcome by stepping in and making sure Congress was working with clear, measurable and accurate facts while debating the issue.

Today, the LCS class is among the largest in the fleet. The industrial base avoided a needless degradation and improvements to the ship's design ensured a more ready Navy.

Committee Assignments Matter

The Senate and House each divide their constitutional oversight of the funding process through myriad committees and subcommittees. Congress has sub-divided its oversight role through the use of such committees, each with varying memberships, terms of office and layers of accountability.

It's important to identify which committees correspond to your issues and pinpoint the Members who sit on those committees. You should also find out which Members are the Chair (committee lead from the Majority Party) and Ranking Member (committee lead from the Minority Party) of your committees of interest. For each committee, there will be two sets of staff members, one for the Majority Party and one for the Minority Party. You should make it a point to know and build relationships with both sides. Over time, the majority shifts back and forth between Republican and Democratic control.

For Your Playbook:

Draw a line down the center of a legal pad. At the top of each column write Republican and Democrat, respectively. On the left margin of the two columns at the top write Senate and halfway down write House. Beneath Senate and House list the relevant committees and Member offices that should care about your issue. Now fill in the names you know from the House and Senate in each category. If you're scratching your head or can only come up with 1 or 2, you need to study up. For an example, go to http://www.capitolintegration.com/3-ringcircus.

The Professional Staff Members (PSMs) who staff the committees and subcommittees in Congress are from both sides of the aisle. Just as the majority party has more seats on a committee or subcommittee, they also have proportionally more staff. A staff director who reports to the Chairperson of the Committee runs the day-to-day operations and leads the PSMs. In appropriations committees, they refer to the staff director as the Clerk of the committee—a nod to earlier times. But don't let the anachronistic moniker fool you, the committee Clerk is an incredibly influential figure. Committee decisions often take place at the staff level, and the Staff Director or Clerk often determines what issues actually need to go before the committee for a vote.

Professional Staff Members (PSMs)

I also want to stress the importance of Professional Staff Members (PSMs). Committee PSMs have significant authority in execution of their duties overseeing a portfolio of interests. Understanding the government agencies, strategies and funding is a central part of their jobs. Members of Congress sitting on the committees often defer to the assessment and judgment of the PSMs. PSMs often determine whether Congress needs to vote on an issue. PSMs exercise significant influence in the form of informal power. Their expertise is widely respected by the committee members they serve.

Example:

In 2004, the Navy wanted to fund a plan to extend the life of the 22-ship TICONDEROGA class of cruisers. The Navy nominally procures ships with an expectation of a 30-year life. During those 30 years, various technologies evolve and often the Navy will introduce or "back fit" them into the existing ships, improving their capability. Various machinery and propulsion systems also must undergo periodic heavy overhaul during the life of the ship. In this case, the Navy proposed a multi-hundred million dollar mid-life repair and upgrade program, beginning with newer ships and working its way back.

Congressional PSMs thought it illogical to upgrade newer ships first, but the Navy was stubborn and didn't change its plan. So Congress cut funding for the cruiser modernization line. PSMs have the expertise and authority to recommend to their voting committee members the most practical solutions. It's a fundamental aspect of Congressional oversight.

While the preceding example highlights a Congressional cut, they also can make line-item additions.

Knowing these influential professionals, and them knowing you, is good for business.

Congressional Caucuses

Within both the House and Senate, groups of Representatives and Senators share common legislative interests. They belong to caucuses based on ideological, policy issue or social contours. Congressional leadership formally recognizes dozens of caucuses. The strength of caucuses lies in the informal power and the influence they exert on relevant issues because of the amplified voice in their numbers. Approaching caucuses with your issue can similarly amplify the voice of your issue.

Member Offices

Senators and Representatives have personal offices for handling state, district and constituent business. The size of the staff varies by several factors. All Senate personal offices have a larger staff than the office of a Congressman, even in states where there is only one at-large Member of Congress, like Montana. A Senate office for a state with a large population such as California or Florida will have a significantly larger staff than a Senate office of a less populated state, like Maine.

The Chief of Staff (COS) is the head of both Senate and House personal offices. The COS typically keeps tabs on the politics of the day, the fundraising, the reelection effort, and of course, the Members' positions on specific issues of interest. In the House, it is also typical for the COS to have his or her own specific, and sometimes large, portfolio, such as National Security or Healthcare. House and Senate personal offices also have a Legislative Director (LD), charged with coordinating all policy efforts. Beneath the LD are the Legislative Assistants (LAs), each responsible for portfolios of activities. In the House, it is common for an LA to handle multiple portfolios, for example, National Security, Veterans and Foreign Policy. Some personal offices have Legislative Correspondents (LCs) and interns who share numerous operational responsibilities and handle constituent services.

It's important to know who is responsible for your issue (product, industry, or policy impact). Do you know exactly who within your Senator or Congressman's office oversees issues that matter to your business? You must identify which staffers look after your issue, and foster relationships with them. If possible, do so even before you need to ask them for help.

For Your Playbook:

Do this today. For AT LEAST the offices of your two senators and one representative. Go online and look up the legislative assistant for your subject. This is easy and will take you five minutes. I'll talk later about how to have a meaningful conversation with that person. Extra credit if you can fill in the blocks of Figure 11 for your representative.

Figure 11: The Intersection of Congressional and Committee Offices

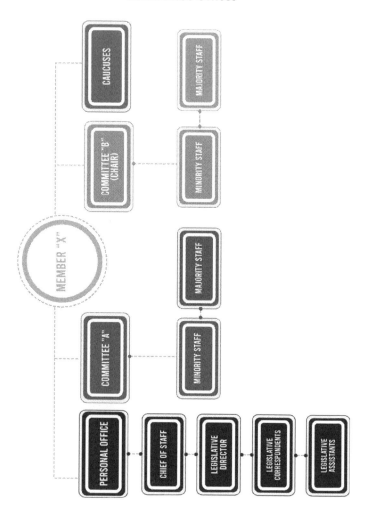

Figure 11 depicts the reality of senators and representatives overseeing multiple formal interests: their own personal office, multiple committees of which they are members and caucuses they have determined warrant their participation. It's common for senators and representatives to serve on as many as four committees and associated subcommittees that are not all shown in Figure 11.

Why Should They Care?

You may ask yourself why a Member of Congress or Congressional staff would make time for you and your business?

It is your job to help make them care.

As the late Speaker of the House Tip O'Neill famously quipped, "All politics is local." Members of Congress and their staffs have an implicit desire to support constituent issues. Your aim is to tell your story in a way that makes it relevant for your audience. If a Congressional office can draw the line between your business and an issue area prominent to their platform, they will want to know you. Drawing this line for them and making sure Congress knows the relevance of your business, technology, idea or policy should be a part of your overall assessment of the business environment.

Example:

While a corporate lobbyist, I represented DRS (now Leonardo SpA) to Congress as part of a supplier base for the Virginia class submarine. Efforts to increase production from one submarine per year to two submarines per year were being jointly pressed by industry and the Navy. Two per year would generate savings for the government in the hundreds of millions of dollars.

DRS had facilities in multiple states that supplied small but significant parts for the submarines. One part was galley refrigerators, made in Missouri. Making the Missouri Congressional delegation care about submarines was easy for DRS—it meant over 100 jobs and millions of dollars per year to the state. Missouri's Congressional delegation had Senators and Representatives serving on relevant committees and in party leadership in both chambers. Their voices and votes carried influence in the debate and decision.

In Chapter 8, you'll learn much more about strategic communications with stakeholders and decision-makers.

Managing the Clock

In Congress, time drives everything. It is critical to understand the value and the role of time management in any Congressional undertaking. The whole outcome of your sale does not necessarily hinge on term limits and election outcomes, but these realities can certainly have an impact and should be in the back of your mind as you orchestrate your sales strategy.

The Congressional Clock:

- A Congressional session spans 2 years. For example, in 2019, we were in the second year of the 116th Congress, which began in 2018.

- Legislation not completed within a 2-year session effectively dies and must be re-introduced in the next Congress.

- Representatives in Congress serve 2-year terms. Every Congressperson is up for re-election every 2 years. If another candidate defeats the Representative you worked with, you must start over with the new Representative.

- Senators serve 6-year terms and are elected in one of three classes. So, every 2 years one-third of US Senators are up for re-election. If your Senator loses their election, you must start over with another Senator.

☐ There are a fixed number of days during which you can complete legislative actions.

☐ Congress measures the time devoted to a particular issue on the floor in hours.

☐ Senators and Representatives must request time and they yield back unused time when speaking on the floor of their chamber.

☐ Senators and Representatives serve on multiple committees of varying relative significance. But there are only a finite number of years that they can serve as the Chair of a committee or subcommittee depending on the importance of the committee.

☐ During committee hearings, rounds of questioning are rigidly divided by as little as 3-minute increments to as much as 10-minutes.

☐ Committee seniority largely depends on time in elected office and time served on that respective committee.

☐ Leadership teams of 3 to 6 Members or Senators of each party lead the House and Senate.

They drive the political messaging and alignment during a specified session of Congress.

I'll explain further how a thorough understanding of the ongoing pressures induced by the clock can weigh on your issue—and how you can be prepared to make the most of your window. For now, I'll step back from the 3 rings as I describe who your federal customer really is in Chapter 5.

Putting it into Practice—The Engagement Strategy

Now that you've gone through the three rings of influence, Figure 12 adds the appropriate contacts from the Congress ring to our growing engagement strategy. You'll now notice that each ring has its own section of the engagement strategy. In the coming chapters I will fill in the greyed-out boxes, to flesh out the engagement strategy. For a template of an engagement plan matrix we use at Capitol Integration, go to www.capitolintegration.com/3-ringcircus.

Figure 12: The Engagement Plan – Part III

ISSUE A (FY 3)	Title			Message	Notes	Contact
Industry						
Bill Jones	VP, Supply Chain			We need to notify suppliers of 3-year forecast	Speaking at Industry Day	Bjones@ prime.com
Terry Smith	Contracting officer			We must be on contract by 1 May		
Agency						
Mr. Big	Asst Secretary			Foreign competition is a concern.		jking@ agency.gov
Mike Richards	Program Mgr			RFP must be issued by 31 Jan		mrichards@ agency.gov
Ms. King	Scheduler/EA				Don't call on Mondays	jking@ agency.gov
Congress						
Lisa Abernathy	HASC PSM			Need to coordinate with Rep Smith's team	Will take meeting before mark	first.last@ mail.house.gov
Roy Willow	Rep. Smith MLA			Need project sheet inputs by 15 Jan	Inputs due March 1st	first.last@ mail.house.gov

Chapter 5: The Balancing Act – The Customer Constellation

"Don't find customers for your products, find products for your customers."
—*Seth Godin*

I once worked with a medium-sized ($100 million in revenue) supplier that had a more reliable and less expensive component than what was installed on a specific class of US Navy ship. Hundreds of inferior components, as measured by failure and repair rates, were installed throughout each vessel. The client wanted the chance to compete for the opportunity to unseat the incumbent and have the US Navy adopt its superior product. However, the prime contractor for the ship class wasn't sufficiently motivated to organize and conduct a competition for every new thing that came along.

Recognizing the client's story was falling on deaf ears, and knowing it had a better solution, together we mapped a communications strategy with Congressional defense committees. Congress always likes to see competition and particularly likes to see companies of all sizes get an equal chance. Congressional staff added specific legislation to the National Defense Authorization Act (NDAA) directing the Navy to conduct competitions wherever possible. The company wasn't seeking a handout; it just wanted a fair chance to compete for the opportunity.

Congressional direction, written into law, is unavoidable. Agencies simply must react to it; it can't be ignored. Recognizing that its customer wasn't just the Big Prime to whom they sold parts helped this client see a bigger picture. Others in its true customer constellation proved quite helpful. I'll talk more about the customer constellation below.

With federal sales, your customer is not the traditional end-user of whatever product you are selling. Your federal customer is the larger groups of people who decide to work with you, buy your product or collaborate on a mutually beneficial policy decision.

Key Term:

"Customer constellation," is a term that we will use throughout the book to reference the array of important individuals that exist throughout and across all three of the Industry, Agency and Congress rings.

Chapters 1 through 3 were about familiarizing you with the important players that exist within the three rings: industry, agency, and Congress. Now, let's redefine those individuals in your mind from sales contacts to your federal customer.

You need to become an expert at reading organization charts.

This applies to the agency you work with, Congressional offices, associations, industry players and any entity that affects your sale. You need to know the hierarchy of personnel, what their associated titles mean and what motivates their actions. These grains of information matter when you initiate outreach and ensure that you are building relationships with the right people.

Most times, organization charts are easily searchable on company or agency websites. But sometimes, federal agencies are more restrictive with what is publicly available, for security concerns and maintaining private information (names, phone numbers and email addresses). Several excellent subscription services keep up-to-date records of the never-ending shuffle of officials within government positions, including Bloomberg Government (BGOV), http://www.bgov.com, and KnowWho, http://www.know-who.com. Investing in a tool that allows you to access the information you need to make the right contacts will pay for itself.

Pro Tip:

Federal phone directories change very little over time. Even though individual people rotate in and out of positions, the phone number assigned to that office almost always remains the same.

The Customer

Your federal customer differs from a business-to-business sale. Here's why:

- Your customer is not one person.

- Your customer is not one entity.

- Your customer is actually a network of individuals across the 3 rings; a constellation of people associated with the buying decisions.

Figure 13: The Generic Federal Customer Network

Figure 13 shows potential contacts within your customer network (starting top moving clockwise): Congress, Agency (ex. Pentagon), Prime Industries, Peers/Board Members, the White House, Congressional Staff Contacts.

Handling the Customer

Interaction with your customer constellation should not be a "one size fits all" approach. Different people throughout your network will require various levels of engagement, sophistication and finesse. This can depend on which ring they fall into, their rank, personality type or any number of other factors. Regardless, treat each individual person as just that—an individual. You must also consider how influential a particular person is to the ultimate outcome of your sale. If the answer is "very important," it behooves you to go the extra mile.

Some situations will call for direct contact: a phone call, email or request for a face-to-face meeting. When using the direct approach, schedule the call or meeting ahead of time. *Do not* cold call and *do not* "drop-in." Both are disrespectful.

On other occasions, your approach might be to coordinate a chance encounter at an association or business event. It's perfectly appropriate to buttonhole a target gently at a public event. "Mr. Smith, great to run into you're here. I'd like to connect with you and your team to discuss project 'X'. Can I follow up with you or reach out to your scheduling assistant to set up a time?" Understated, professional, respectful. You don't brief them on the fly at the event. Just ask for the follow-up. You'll get it.

There may also be times when you enter from the side or from the top down in the organization chart. If you already know someone else in the agency or that individual's boss, an introduction can pave the way for you. Be judicious. Be thoughtful. Be mindful of the timing.

You may find it useful to let a third party convey a message on your behalf. The third party in this case might be an author who writes for a relevant professional periodical. It might also be an association official who keynotes an event or moderates a professional panel. There's no reason you can't connect with that official before an event to educate and inform them of your issue or interest.

You may determine that you need to hire extra help to gain a specific access or capability. There are hired guns out there that specialize in brokering relationships between third parties and the agencies they formerly worked for. It may be worth considering, but only in moderation. Their reach is usually limited.

Over-communicating is perhaps the worst mistake amateurs can make. This includes communicating too frequently throughout the process or at inappropriate times. Bringing forward an idea or issue at the wrong time, when your audience can't do anything about it, wastes everyone's time. Don't be an amateur. Commit to understanding the underlying process running throughout the 3-ring Circus.

But, how do you know which method to apply in which situation? If you aren't working according to a plan, you may not know.

Unfortunately, people can usually, if not always, tell when you don't have a plan. And trust me, if they detect you are working off-the-cuff, they will not go out of their way to tell you. It just makes you look bad and the odds of them helping you low. Working your contact log only when the CRM system tells you it's time to check in will be entirely ineffective. You will approach both the right and the wrong people at the wrong time.

Example:

I work with a research and development company who developed a cutting-edge method of underwater diver communications. The client was communicating directly with a program office at the US Special Operations Command (SOCOM). While their SOCOM customer contact had an important role in the decision to move forward, that customer contact was but one of several with a role in the actual decision. Continuing to press on the same contact, knock on the same door, and leave messages for the same person wasn't helping the client.

The company hired me to expand the engagement plan and sharpen the message. Helping the client see the rest of the customer constellation helped advance the technology and drew on the positive inputs of others in the same network.

Does this look familiar?

- Your request for a meeting goes unanswered.

- You are granted a meeting and recognize quickly that the individual across the table is listening but not engaging.

- You have a slide deck that you are determined to get through because you want to convey every last important point.

- The person across the table from you looks at her watch at the 29-minute mark and has to wrap it up; no time for questions.

- You don't get the follow-up meeting.

- Your government customer answers a hearing question with a response that tinges your proposal, product or policy.

- The latest RFP is issued and the contents catch you by surprise.

- The bill comes out and Congress did not address your issue at all; not a single word you suggested made it in the bill language.

- If any of these scenarios apply, it is likely that you have, unwittingly, misplayed your role in the process. This could be the result of one unfortunate misstep, but most likely the by-product of misalignment throughout the whole process.

To avoid these unpleasant outcomes, you need a plan.

Making a Plan

Within the business-to-business selling method, you will often hear mention of business decision mapping. It looks like this:

- Identify the prospect.

- Learn the strategy and motivations of the prospect.

- Determine the buyer at the prospect entity (industry or agency).

- Perceive who influences or enables the buyer.

- Understand who has what decision-making authority.

- Spot who actually executes the order.

How does this concept transfer to the federal space? Who is the decision-maker? It is likely several people I identified across the three rings of influence.

But, it's not just a matter of identifying who the players might be. You need to think about how to educate them and influence their thinking. This is where decision mapping transposes on top of the 3 rings. Within and across the industry, agency and Congress rings there are **Gatekeepers, Influencers, Enablers and Decision Makers.**

Figure 14: Who Decides?

- Gatekeepers
  - Schedulers
  - Contract Officers
  - Staff Assistants

- Influencers
  - Peers
  - Third-party Advocates
  - Associations
  - Constituents

- Enablers
  - Deputies
  - "Informal" Leaders
  - Thought Leaders
  - Congressional Staff Members
  - Professional/Committee Staff Members

- Decision Maker
  - Political appointees
  - Senior Executive Service
  - General/Flag Officers
  - "Senior" Officers
  - Program Executives

Starting to sound like three-dimensional chess? It can be. But you can master it.

My system is to assign each contact in your customer constellation a label that signifies their decision-mapping role. Are they a Gatekeeper, someone who opens the door? An Influencer, someone who can nudge your project in the right direction? An Enabler, someone who is instrumental in getting your product to the end goal? Or, a Decision Maker, the person whose signature is on the dotted line?

Figure 14 shows some examples of which positions/job titles tend to fill the different decision mapping areas. Keep in mind that while this figure is a perfect example of one-to-one alignment between a contact and a spot on the decision map, it is possible for the same person to occupy multiple categories. For example, someone could be both an influencer and an enabler. A gatekeeper can also have influence. There are endless combinations.

Example:

Throughout my time in federal sales, I have interacted with many Schedulers in Capitol Hill offices. A Scheduler is a prime example of a star in your customer constellation that could be a Gatekeeper, or much more.

Some Schedulers, true to their title, really do just schedule meetings and appointments for the office staff and Members of Congress themselves. That makes them a Gatekeeper; they will literally get you in the door. Others, whom I have worked with, have been with their particular office for years. They have the full confidence of the Chief of Staff and the trust of the Member. This type of staffer is a Gatekeeper and an Influencer. Treat them as such, and you will get much farther.

In one situation, I was attempting to have a Senator visit a client event. Per the Senator's calendar, he was not available as he was committed to an event across town. However, since the Scheduler knew me (and the client) and understood the relationship, she found a way to "double book" the Senator. Those situations can go either way. By knowing the dynamics of the relationships in both directions, everyone can win: Senator, Scheduler and you!

With this new perspective on your customer, perhaps you realize that your contact plan up to now has been less than optimal. But before you can fix that problem, we need to discuss the constraints under which your customer constellation works. These limitations fully inform what your customers can do within their defined roles and what you should reasonably expect from them.

In Part II, I'll walk you through the mechanics of the budget process and methods to help you better communicate within its confines.

Putting it into Practice — The Engagement Strategy

Now, it's time to fill in those missing areas in the engagement strategy. This is where you have an opportunity physically label your customer constellation with their decision-mapping role. This final piece allows you to hone your pitch, time your outreach and maximize your outcomes. For a template of an engagement plan matrix we use at Capitol Integration, go to **www.capitolintegration.com/about**.

Figure 15: The Engagement Plan – Part IV

ISSUE A (FY 3)	Title	Gatekeeper	Influencer	Enabler	Decision Maker	Message	Notes	Contact
Industry								
Bill Jones	VP, Supply Chain				X	We need to notify suppliers of 3-year forecast	Speaking at Industry Day	Bjones@prime.com
Terry Smith	Contracting officer	X	X			We must be on contract by 1 May		
Agency								
Mr. Big	Asst Secretary .				X	Foreign competition is a concern		jking@agency.gov
Mike Richards	Program Mgr		X	X		RFP must be issued by 31 Jan		mrichards@agency.gov
Ms. King	Scheduler/EA	X	X				Don't call on Mondays	jking@agency.gov
Congress								
Lisa Abernathy	HASC PSM		X	X	X	Need to coordinate with Rep Smith's team	Will take meeting before mark	first.last@mail.house.gov
Roy Willow	Rep. Smith MLA		X			Need project sheet inputs by 15 Jan	Inputs due March 1st	first.last@mail.house.gov

PART II:
The Main Acts

Chapter 6: The Flaming Hoops Act—Moving a Budget

"No Money shall be drawn from the Treasury, but in Consequence of Appropriations made by Law; and a regular Statement and Account of the Receipts and Expenditures of all public Money shall be published from time to time."

—The United States Constitution, Article I, Section 9, Clause 7

A small research and development company with fewer than 10 employees had successfully garnered a Small Business Innovation Research (SBIR) contract with the US Special Operations Command (SOCOM). They recognized a potential commercial market for their technology, but the SBIR rules didn't allow for the technology to be sold commercially without a difficult-to-obtain waiver. Company leaders knew their SOCOM customer well and were well respected within their industry. They just didn't know the Congressional ring well.

The company came to me to improve their situation. Together we mapped an engagement plan of interested Congressional stakeholders. We coordinated questions being asked of the SOCOM program office and small business office by Congressional staff—applying gentle external force to the agency bureaucracy.

The Power of the Purse

The clause above relays the most important thing to know about the federal budget process: Congress must approve every single dollar spent.

There are no exceptions: Congress approves all federal funding.

Congress approves federal money by passing authorization and appropriations legislation. These bills dole out federal dollars to be spent on various programs and services throughout the government. When the government agrees to pay for a product or service with federally approved money, it is called the obligation of funds. The most typical vehicle for an obligation of funds is a federal contract.

Federal contracts are the tether that pull Congress directly into your customer constellation.

Congress has a permanent connection to your business if you hope to sell at the federal level. It has been this way since the founding of our country.

Don't ignore it or fight it—embrace this reality. It can be a game changer for you.

The Budget Process

The good news is that the formulation of the federal budget is fairly simple. The process is designed to be deliberate, sequential and s-l-o-w. Compared to how you derive your business financial plan over days or weeks, the federal budgeting process takes years. There are three basic phases: Planning and Programming, Legislating and Execution (see Figure 16). Note: I've taken some artistic license in simplifying how the budget is developed to aid your understanding and retention.

Figure 16: The Phases of the Budget Process

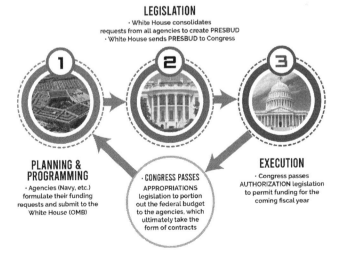

LEGISLATION
· White House consolidates requests from all agencies to create PRESBUD
· White House sends PRESBUD to Congress

1

2

3

PLANNING &
PROGRAMMING
· Agencies (Navy, etc.)
formulate their funding
requests and submit to the
White House (OMB)

· CONGRESS PASSES
APPROPRIATIONS
legislation to portion
out the federal budget
to the agencies, which
ultimately take the
form of contracts

EXECUTION
· Congress passes
AUTHORIZATION legislation
to permit funding for the
coming fiscal year

Planning and Programming

To kick off the process, every government agency (see Chapter 3) develops a budget request for the coming fiscal year. Each agency has its own internal process for planning the budget. The Department of Defense has the most robust process, known as the Planning Programming and Budgeting System (PPBS). PPBS stems from a concept pioneered in the 1960s of using analysis to identify and measure programs that meet required needs. You read that correctly—the 1960s.

PPBS has more steps—
Figure 16 is what you need to know.

Legislation

Agencies complete their budget proposal and then send the requests to the Office of Management and Budget (OMB). OMB is part of the Executive Branch and is the largest of the President's Executive Offices. OMB's job is to gather all the agency budget requests and assemble them into one government-wide budget input for the President to review. After the President's Office has submitted any additions or changes, OMB repackages the final product into the official President's Budget (PB). It is what the President would like to see funded for the coming fiscal year; *it is a request*. Many think of the PB as a political document because not only is it a rationale for funding the government, it reflects the priorities of the current administration.

Once Congress has the PB, Members of Congress confer within the various committees and subcommittees to determine what to fund and what to cut. Congress ultimately conceives its own budget plan and drafts corresponding legislation to enact it. Assuming Congress passes the necessary bills, they can then distribute, or appropriate, the approved sum of money amongst the federal agencies.

Execution

Acts of budget execution refer to those steps associated with departments of government allocating, obligating and spending *funds appropriated by Congress*.

The Budget Clock

The budget preparation process takes place over the course of years. OMB submits the budget for a given year to Congress by the first Monday in February, allowing enough time for Congressional committees to review, modify and approve legislative outcomes before the beginning of the upcoming fiscal year on October 1st.

I will dedicate Part III to discussing how the timing of the budget process can and should affect your business strategy. For now, let's focus on the budget contents themselves.

Inputs and Outputs

The original budget documents created by the agencies and OMB were the "input." The funding bills passed by Congress are the legislative "output" of the budget process.

As I said above, each government department (DHS, DoD, VA, etc.) makes their own budget submission to OMB. Some budgets are more detailed than others. DoD, for example, incorporates specific supporting tables of information and breaks down each funding category to detail where funding will go. Along with the tables are exhibits that outline recent funding history and, to a lesser extent, future funding projections and estimates.

Each department has developed its method over years of give and take among the agency, OMB and Congress. Budget materials often include words designed to message the strategic or specific direction of an agency or department on a variety of funding choices. Further, and specific to DoD, justifications or "J-books" contain supplemental and relevant details surrounding the proposed spending plan. Other departments, such as Treasury, include far less specificity in their budget input, relying on the ongoing dialogue with Congressional staff to fill in the details. All these methods of budget input work to the same end.

Do Your Homework

Once submitted to Congress, budget documents are available for public review. Exceptions apply to classified funding for the "three letter agencies" (FBI, CIA, NSA). And within DoD, like the three-letter agencies, sections of the budget remain classified. DoD refers to those sections as the "black" budget.

Understanding what is in the budget input to OMB and Congress can inform your business strategy. As suggested in Chapter 3, many decision makers within program offices are not well versed in the details surrounding the budget input for their own program. It's inexcusable, but true.

However, it is equally inexcusable for you to not know the relevant details of the budget affecting your program or product. Those details are readily available for you to read, review and analyze. Most departments post the public budget materials in a searchable format online. Sometimes the information is buried under a few layers of the agency website, but a simple web browser search of "FYxx budget materials" will quickly point you in the right direction. You don't have to read the thousands of pages in the document. Simply search for the keywords related to your topic of interest—e.g., missile, border or tariff.

A surprising number of businesspeople fail to do this small bit of homework that will make a world of difference for their bottom line. Don't miss this easy opportunity to get ahead of the curve.

For Your Playbook:

Put down the book. Go to your online search tool. Type in "Budget Materials FY20 Defense." Click on the government website that comes up (DoD Comptroller). Click on any pdf on the page. You have just opened a treasure chest of information. Now, do the same thing for the agency you wish to do business with. Dig in.

The Comparison Game

When reviewing budget documents surrounding your programs of interest or capability, one of the most useful things you can do is compare budgets across fiscal years. This can often inform your fundamental business strategy. Comparing between years will help you track trends over time and give you a much better sense of your operating environment. Also, noting changes in the spending plan from year to year will tell you a lot about which programs are moving forward. What's requested this year that wasn't in the forecast last year?

The decision to fund, or not fund, is not accidental. It reflects current priorities.

Several services and professionals report major trends and detail program shifts. Bloomberg Government (BGOV), PoliticoPro, McAleese & Associates and Cypress International all have sound research teams and produce high caliber products. The minor investment in these services is well worth it. They track the big picture, which can have a big impact on your strategy to win the contract.

While this sounds like tedious and time consuming work, it's far easier than you might imagine. Once you've established the practice of incorporating budget materials into your business intelligence, it becomes routine. The final public documents for each fiscal year are only posted once per year, in predictable proximity to the movement of the PB to Congress (early February or March). What might be a few hours of research for you can pay dividends in strategic value throughout the year. Inevitably, once you become familiar with these documents, you'll find multiple reasons to refer back to them and incorporate the information into your internal strategic planning.

You have access to on-the-ground resources about your program at every step in the budget process. Knowledge is power.

Chapter 7: The Human Cannonball—Out Comes a Bill

"You don't get rich off your day job. You get rich off your homework."
—Daymond John

A small startup (5 employees) based in Washington, DC, figured out that the manner in which the Department of Veteran's Affairs tracked and shared mortgage information among the department, banks and loan applicants for its very popular VA loans was horribly antiquated. Company leaders knew they could provide state-of-the-art data sharing and communications capabilities in the form of widely accepted mobile app technology. When this innovation was presented to the VA, it had no interest in acknowledging the problem, let alone pursuing an improved solution. The "not invented here" sign was visible.

We mapped the Congressional ring of the customer constellation and developed support with the Committees on Veterans Affairs as well as the Financial Services Committees. Sometimes agencies are paralyzed and must be told by Congress to move in a particular direction. The VA culture was stuck and needed a push. Congress included report language directing the VA to improve its use of these technologies.

For this startup, this is an example of how venturing into a previously unexplored ring of influence (in this case located just blocks away) produced a meaningful change in its position with the VA.

Bills, Bills, Bills

Let's revisit the policy process timeline. Notice that there is a large chunk of the process, right in the middle, that stands between your product/service and its delivery to an end user. This area is the "Congress phrase."

Figure 17: Policy Process Timeline

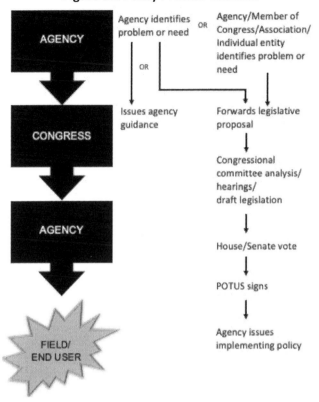

Up to this point, I have focused primarily on the development of authorization and appropriations legislation. As we've covered, these are the funding bills that Congress drafts in response to the PB (President's Budget for those who skipped ahead). But, besides the funding bills, Congress also drafts legislation solely focused on policy. Bills dealing with taxes or trade are examples of legislation with far-reaching policy implications. These policy bills can have a significant impact on your business. You must understand how they are developed, passed and implemented.

Many people subconsciously view the Congress portion of the process as a black hole. They'll watch their issue go into the Capitol Hill vortex on one side and just wait to see what pops out on the other side. This path of disengagement with the process does a huge disservice to your business. You need to make sure you're able to pull your issue through the legislation phase in Congress to the contract stage. This requires active participation on your part and a detailed understanding of the bills affecting you.

I won't pretend to make you a legislative expert with this book, but I can make you conversant enough that you can correctly follow the state of play as it unfolds. Countless additional steps, side steps, workarounds and short circuits can come into play, but they would take us well beyond the scope of what will typically concern your business pursuit. So, let's break it down a bit.

You are most interested in three types of bills: policy, authorization and appropriations.

- **Policy bills** usually address an issue of the day with a political or international element. Think trade, foreign affairs or taxes. Policy bills rarely deal with the actual expenditure of funds.

- **Authorization bills** authorize spending. An authorization bill can also be a policy bill, but if this is the case it will usually only address one department or agency. For example, the National Defense Authorization Act (NDAA) authorizes defense spending, but also addresses a myriad of defense-related policy issues: personnel and pay, procurement guidelines and suggestive and directive language to agencies.

- **Appropriations bills** appropriate, allocate, apportion or distribute the money amongst the agencies. Remember in Chapter 6 when we talked about the obligation of funds? Appropriations bills are the trigger that allows funds to be obligated. Think of an appropriations bill as a bank account for federal agencies, a place to issue checks and withdrawals.

Authorization bills allow the spending.
Appropriations bills do the spending.

Figure 18: How a Bill Becomes a Law

The outcome of the legislative process is the set of bills to which both chambers of Congress (House and Senate) agree, and the President signs into law. These legislative results represent Congress' mark on the President's budget request.

Step-by-Step

1. **Introduction.** Any Congressperson or Senator may introduce a bill. Bills are most commonly introduced on the chamber floor using a prescribed protocol specific to each chamber. The bill is referred to the appropriate committee of jurisdiction.

2. **Committee Stage.** Subcommittees within committees discuss and debate the merits of legislation. They conduct hearings with expert witnesses drawn from government, industry or academia, as appropriate. After a suitable period of review, subcommittees vote to advance the legislation to the full committee or committee of the whole. The full committee then votes to either advance the legislation to the floor or, it dies in committee.

3. **Floor Stage.** When the bill arrives at the floor, it is then open for debate and amendment by the entire chamber. Managers and parliamentarians review amendment proposals to determine whether they are "germane." According to parliamentary rules, only amendments deemed germane are eligible for consideration. Otherwise, the process

would be chaos. For some bills, the floor stage moves quickly. For big bills, such as defense policy and spending, the process can take days and weeks. After the House and Senate each pass their version of the bill on the floor, it proceeds to a conference.

4. **Conference.** During the conference, conferees designated by House and Senate leadership meet to hammer out the differences in the bills and agree to one bill as the conferenced bill.

5. **A conferenced bill** then goes to the House and Senate floors for a final vote of passage.

6. **Presidential Signature**. Congress forwards the bill passed by both the House and Senate to the President for signature or veto. The President has ten days to take action on the bill.

The Media Circus

Along the way to the passage and publication of these bills, flashy headlines attempt to capture the process as it develops: the good, the bad and the ugly. In a continuous news cycle, reporters rarely convey context accurately. In my experience, even highly respected news outlets such as Politico, Bloomberg and The Hill misuse these terms. It is easy for even an experienced person to mistake one thing for another because of inaccurate or incomplete reporting. Bills are generally reported with a few exemplary flashpoints and rarely mention the program(s), funding or policy matters directly impacting your issue.

The good news is bills are released to the public and available in full for anyone to review. You must read the relevant portions of the bills affecting your business as they move through the legislative process. If you don't, you are missing out on a critical aspect of your planning process

Bills reveal A LOT.

Bills convey specific policy guidance, detailed funding approval or disapproval.

The Hearings

Often, bills are partly revealed, prior to their final passage, throughout the subcommittee and committee hearings. Some hearings are classified, but others are public.

Hearings offer an opportunity for Members of Congress to get witnesses on record by responding to questions under oath. Sometimes Members attempt to highlight a constituent interest—a company, product or circumstance that exists in their district or state. Sometimes Members try to get a witness to publicly agree or disagree with an administration policy or aim.

You can actually help staff write relevant questions for their senator or representative to ask. You can suggest questions with a particularly helpful tone or point of view woven into them. Staff members are generally happy to have someone who cares give them input. Not only are you looking out for your interest, you're saving that staffer time and accelerating a good government outcome. Helping connect the dots of government need, business solution and Congressional oversight and support is exactly what people like me do every day. I help make the connections by using the process to the advantage of all.

Agency officials invited or designated to testify before hearings are relatively senior in rank and stature and usually are fully prepared. Many times, they are experienced in the ways of Washington, DC and understand hearings have the potential to be theatrical. It is common practice for agency Congressional liaison officials to solicit the questions in advance. It wouldn't be a stretch to say half of the questions and answers in public testimony are known before the hearing.

Again, the point is not to catch anyone in a "gotcha!" moment or reveal a smoking gun. *The point is to get official positions on the record*. Members of Congress use hearing testimonies to justify their proposed marks to the PB. Hearings are your chance to help the Members advocating for your position get statements on the record that will support any marks they made in favor of your business. Recorded testimony from a third-party issue expert packs a much more powerful punch than the word of one Representative.

You might think knowing half the questions in advance offers a real advantage to the witnesses. It does. But it also means half of the questions are still up for grabs. Half of the questions are asked in the moment by Members of Congress or are follow-ups to a line of questioning revealing a new thread of inquiry.

Example:

I have a client that manufactures a critical technology used in tracking submarines operating in very deep water. The government spends hundreds of millions of dollars annually on this capability.

When a single budget line exceeds $200 million, it risks drawing scrutiny from others looking for their own project funding. There is tremendous competition over funding for such large projects because that kind of money spent in a single Congressional district translates directly into jobs.

During the Chief of Naval Operations' annual budget testimony before the House Armed Services Committee, the Representative representing the district where my client has its principal plant, and who sits on the committee, asked the Admiral if he saw a need to maintain this capability in the national interest. Note: he did not blatantly ask, "Do we need more of product x?"

The Admiral confirmed the criticality and value of the technology, which the Congressman knew could only be provided by the product made in his district. It surprised no one that the question was asked. *The question was asked because I coordinated its wording in advance with the Congressman's staff.* It surprised no one in how it was answered. The key outcome of that hearing was getting the Chief of Naval Operations on record supporting continued funding for a program embedded in the President's Budget request. After that testimony, the likelihood of full funding, or even an add, was improved. Think of it as a form of risk management for your business.

Answer the following questions:

- Do you know who sits on the committees of interest that oversee your agency or program of interest?

- Do you know who your members of Congress are and on what committees and subcommittees they sit?

- Do you follow the schedule of hearings of committees and subcommittees of interest?

〡〡 Do you know where to find them?

〡〡 Do you review transcripts of hearings of interest? Did you know they are posted online, sometimes the same day but usually within 48 hours of the hearing at www.thomas.gov?

If you're unsure of the answers, you're at a disadvantage. Part of your overall plan must be a legislative engagement plan, complete with known Influencers, Enablers, and Decision Makers. You can participate in this essential part of the process.

Tracking Bill Progress

It's both useful and important to know the differences on the way to a final bill, comparing the President's input (PB) with Congressional marks (legislative outputs) of the relevant committees. You can compare exact lines and categories of funding: PB is the input; the mark is the first look at the output. Even in the midst of the process, you may have additional opportunities to revisit a mark before the bill goes from subcommittee to full committee, or from full committee to a conference with the other chamber. There are rules about what you can do and when. But for every rule there are also ways to address special circumstances.

Example:

The Predator drone system came into its own in the post-9/11 era and heralded the introduction of an entirely new industry of unmanned technologies in combat.

Predator was used for surveillance in the early days of the Iraq war. First with the CIA, then with traditional ground forces, variations of arming the Predator drone delivered a new form of standoff-armed conflict. Strikes could take place with much less risk to military personnel on the ground.

Witness testimony during multiple defense hearings as the war ramped up confirmed the facts on the ground: We needed more of this capability, and fast.

Having a solid record of testimony reinforced an operational need that was clearly outpacing the traditional requirements and resourcing process. As a result, Congress jump-started the unmanned aerial drone race by providing substantial additional funding beyond what had been programmed into a budget developed over a year earlier.

Permission to Proceed

With a bill approved by Congress and signed into law by the President, the acquisition world is given the green light. The agency now has permission to implement law with policy. That means the agency can spend money on your product or service.

If you've been watching and participating throughout the process, the bill contains no surprises. You not only know exactly what to expect, you can be the one to provide better, and more accurate, information about the final bill to your agency or Prime customer. For example:

- Did the House or Senate cut your program? Or did both?

- Is there restrictive, suggestive or directive language in the bill?

- Is there a requirement for a "report to Congress" due from the agency within a stated time period?

Agencies will sometimes bristle at changes imposed by Congress. They might ask, rhetorically, "How do they think they know more than we do about this?"

Here's the answer: *it doesn't matter, it just is*. This system teeters on a dynamic tension rod between Congress and the Executive. The results are never perfect and will rarely make everyone happy.

Your goal is to understand and take advantage of the process, not to rationalize it for others.

Chapter 8: The Juggling Act—How to Shape Outcomes

"If you want to influence people, you want them to accept your suggestions…it will be welcomed much more if you have a gentle touch than if you are aggressive."
—Ruth Bader Ginsburg

A large prime with a program in the budget valued at more than $200 million dollars annually was attempting to broaden its product offerings for a different part of the US Navy. The company had been collaborating with other companies on a classified developmental project. Each had its own relationships to the US Navy customer. It became clear that working together, developmental costs could be shared and the concept could proceed faster.

Two companies worked together, appearing alongside each other, explaining to both US Navy customers and Congressional staff the value that was within reach if funding could be accelerated. Congress, with the Navy's concurrence, added several million dollars to the developmental effort, thereby accelerating a significant capability to the ultimate end user—sailors in the fleet.

In this case, industry, agency and Congressional rings of influence were all aligned to produce a good government solution at a faster pace. This was a win for everyone.

Shape It Up

Part I covered *who* you need to be targeting with your federal sale. Chapter 5 introduced the concept of a customer constellation and how to orchestrate a decision-mapping scheme within your federal customer network. Now, for the *how* to best communicate with those contacts, to shape outcomes that will benefit your business.

Interspersed throughout what appears to be a strictly serial budget and acquisition processes are opportunities for you to engage with your customer constellation: those people who influence, enable or make decisions affecting your issue.

Key Term:

"Shaping" is a colloquialism for solving a government need while shifting the advantage to your business. Shaping is about applying influence at the right time to increase the odds that the government customer will recognize and fund your idea.

Influencing, Selling and Lobbying. What's the Difference?

When I speak of influence, I'm referring to you using your communications skills to educate and inform people who should care about your issue. Most of us are undisciplined in our communications. We think out loud far more often than we realize. That bad habit stems from not preparing adequately for the opportunity to speak. I'll share a simple tool to help tighten your words and thoughts. But first, a little more on influence.

Influencing often gets a bad rap because people associate it negatively with lobbying. Unfortunately, a few lobbyists in the past abused their role and acted outside the law, staining public perception of the practice. Because of a few bad apples, the general notion became that Washington, DC is a "swamp" and "the whole place is corrupt" because of lobbyists.

The fact is, using your communications skills to influence an outcome is lobbying. That's okay. Lobbying has been a part of our government culture since the nation's inception. According to the Center for Responsive Politics, the term "lobbying" stems from our British forbears when Parliament would use forceful exchanges during sessions.

You may be asking yourself, why are we talking about this? Who cares about lobbying and what does it have to do with my federal business?

If you don't properly disclose lobbying activity when in fact you are lobbying, your business could be subject to a fine of *up to $200,000 per instance.* Some salespeople think that their behaviors do not constitute lobbying, and as a result fail to legally report their activities; it's called failing to disclose. Further, overhead charges worked into your government pricing can't include the costs of lobbying activity. Doing so can result in you retroactively restating your books, profit and earnings. How bad a day would that be for you?

Very clear and specific rules govern lobbying communications. The Lobbying Disclosure Act (LDA) clearly defines lobbying and who in the government qualifies as a covered official. Covered officials are those "covered" by the LDA. Depending on the seniority of the government official with whom you engage, and how often you engage with them, it is very possible you are lobbying under the stipulations of the LDA. If you interact with anyone who fits the category of a "covered official," you must understand the reporting implications in accordance with the LDA. To learn more about the LDA, check out the House website under the Public Disclosure tabs (https://lobbyingdisclo-sure.house.gov/amended_lda_guide.html).

Example:

I attended the annual meeting of the Ship-builder's Council of America (SCA). At the evening cocktail party, the chatter was about a shipyard that had just won a somewhat large contract with an agency. A retired Admiral, hired to run the Washington DC office of the shipyard, commented that he didn't lobby and didn't intend to register to lobby.

On its face, I found it an absurd statement. Surely, he was engaged at the highest echelons of government within his daily duties. It seemed a risky move. In my view, such a high-profile person, overseeing the win of a significant contract, not registering as a lobbyist or his activity as lobbying was preposterous.

It turns out his company actually had registered him to lobby. Perhaps he didn't know his people were looking out for him. Regardless, his public words didn't align with reality, and could have been extremely problematic had he not been registered.

Don't give your credibility away. Know the rules and live by them.

The moral of the story is: Don't be afraid or dissuaded by the term lobbyist. Advocating to the federal government on behalf of your business is a good thing, just understand the regulations behind your actions and report them accordingly.

How You Communicate

All companies, large and small, have equal access to the people who determine the fate of a sale or assignment of a contract. Don't think just because you're a small company that you can't engage those who determine your fate. Similarly, don't think just because you're a large company that you can roll in roughshod.

If you're part of a larger company with many communicators, your messaging must be consistent and aligned. Most large companies have rules about who is allowed to conduct visits with particular individuals within the customer constellation. Subtlety and finesse can go a long way regardless of your size. Your federal customers keep track of what was said by whom year over year.

A consistent and well-told story will distinguish you and your company.

Excuse the coming generalization: Many company presidents, business developers and salespeople either communicate to excess or communicate poorly when interacting within the 3-ring circus. Especially within the agency ring and Congress ring.

It doesn't matter whether you are pitching a new and improved widget or a new way to conquer space travel. Your issue and recommended action must be tight and concise. Think *Shark Tank*, without the celebrities and editing. When scheduling meetings with the people you have so carefully worked to identify and approach, make the absolute most of the opportunity. Let's look at some channels and methods of communicating.

Work Smart, Not Harder

Applying influence through your communication style is a long game. Working one path to reach one significant individual isn't enough. Remember, the customer constellation and the decision mapping we outlined in our engagement strategy spreadsheet. This is where you need to embrace your role as the "ringmaster" of the 3-ring circus. Among many moving parts and people, it is your job to conduct a thoughtful, rhythmic, purposeful means of messaging and communications that weave together to achieve one desired outcome or outcomes (i.e., a Plan B, or second-best scenario).

There's only so much time and bandwidth to devote to any aspect of the sale. Smart and thoughtful communications are force multipliers.

Making sure that your messaging and means make the optimal use of your resources will ultimately make you more effective. Again, work smart, not harder.

Figure 19: Reaching Your Desired Outcome

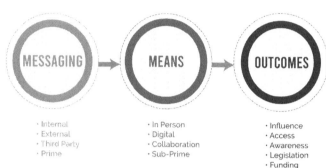

- Internal
- External
- Third Party
- Prime

- In Person
- Digital
- Collaboration
- Sub-Prime

- Influence
- Access
- Awareness
- Legislation
- Funding

Outcomes: Begin With The End

Your engagement strategy should begin with the desired outcome in mind. But, you also need to make sure you can deliver on your promises. Ask yourself these questions before pursuing a federal sale:

1. Is your product/service/capability something that the government needs, wants or maybe doesn't know it needs?

2. Will it truly improve the condition of the government agency as seen in the eyes of its end user?

Example:

One of my clients successfully garnered Congressional support for a program the Navy wanted to enhance. The company had positioned itself with the Navy as the only source capable of delivering a desired technical solution.

For a few years in a row, the client, in full coordination with the Navy, was able to increase and accelerate funding by amplifying Congressional support. Often when Congress shows support for a program, the agency will follow suit and expand its budget request in subsequent years. But in this case, the Navy didn't.

This was a clear signal the Navy was no longer interested in growing my client's program. Instead of adjusting to the Navy's decision, the client wanted to go back to Congress and repeat its request for increased funding. I let the client know we could not continue to pursue this. It was no longer good government. In this case, I fired the client.

You can't push something on a government agency that the agency has fairly assessed and determined they don't want. At that point, you are no longer improving their condition; you're wasting your time and taxpayer dollars. Overall, it's a bad look and an imprudent strategy.

Protect your reputation by acting in the interest of good government. In the long run it will pay off.

Improving Customer Intimacy

There are a lot of ways you can find out what your federal customer needs. This is particularly easy if you are maintaining sufficient communication with them. Customer intimacy is a colloquialism for what some might refer to as emotional IQ. Do you get them? Do you understand their culture; their operational needs?

Your desired outcome could take multiple forms:

- Funding for your product.

- Favorable policy outcomes.

- Supportive legislative language.

- Adoption of your technologies.

- Becoming part of an ongoing relationship.

- Enhanced credibility among your customer constellation.

- A permanent position in a particular supply chain.

- Recognition as a credible expert in an area of mutual interest.

Does your customer understand your desired outcome and can they repeat it back to you or others?

Your ability to test this confirms your level of customer intimacy.

Messaging: Five Ways, One Goal

A cohesive messaging strategy can be among your most critical instruments towards leveraging your desired outcome.

Are all of your messages, messaging paths, actions and methods working toward your ideal outcome? They should. In fact, your desired outcome should be at the heart of any messaging or engagement strategy your business conducts.

Let's consider five components of your business's messaging matrix:

1. Internal messaging

2. External messaging

3. Third party advocacy

4. Communication with your prime

5. Communication as a prime

How well do these areas align with your end goal?

Figure 20: Messaging: 5 Ways, One Goal

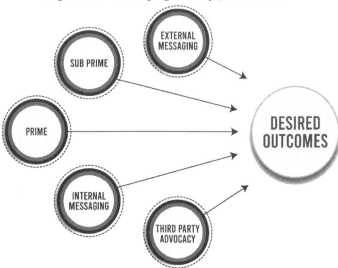

1. Internal Messaging

- Is there a real corporate strategy in place?

- Is it understood by your employees?

- How is it communicated?

- Is it funded?

- Do authorities align with accountabilities?

- Do employees know what particular outcomes mean to the company?

2. External Messaging

- Are you or your leadership participating in relevant associations to the correct degree?

- To what degree is your company or technology known within your industry?

- What do the outward facing employees say to their peers and counterparts? How do you know?

- Are you a thought leader on policy?

- Are you seen as supporting your customer or challenging your customer?

- Do you participate in trade shows, or walk the floor networking?

- Does your intended audience understand your message?

- Do you or company representatives present at symposia or professional conferences?

- Do you advertise in media your customer goes to for information? Trade magazines, association flyers, mailings and LinkedIn groups?

3. Third Party Advocacy

- Does your advocate clearly understand convey your message?

- How much leeway does your advocate have in deeper discussions about your message?

- You can reach out to panelists before a trade show or seminar to discuss issues of common interest. Doing so can allow you to share a point of view. You can't control what a panelist says, but you can attempt to engage them in advance.

- You or a ghostwriter can be published in trade journals, newsletters and blogs. Every outlet is eager to receive inputs of legitimate content.

- Are your advocates really advocates? They may have multiple loyalties or conflicting interests based on their ever-changing client roster.

- You have the ability to engage think tank analysts, industry reporters and thought leaders. It's much easier than you might think.

- Third parties often have more in common with your perspective than not. Influencing messages in these forums requires your active participation.

You can make a difference in the ongoing conversation, sometimes without personally uttering the words. Here are a few examples of channels that allow for many voices carrying your one message:

- Authors for hire exist across all industries.

- Think tanks of all persuasions can be brought under contract and often offer a menu of options to provide mutual benefit.

- Association newsletters, magazines and digital content.

- Panels and panelists at public events.

- Keynote speakers.

Example:

In my corporate government relations role, think tanks would regularly request a meeting to discuss mutual interests. Think tanks come in many shapes and sizes and generally have some ideological contours: conservative, progressive, etc. They typically get their funding through industry subscriptions, corporate donations and philanthropic endowments.

It's common for think tanks to offer companies a menu of events, seminars, retreats and panels to which they might choose to subscribe for a fee. This is where think tanks make money. Fees can be in the hundreds of thousands of dollars per year. This is a good investment for companies because they are assured of having access to a host of highly credible messengers.

Having qualified and credible third party advocates tout your program or capability can help enhance your marketing and reach. While smaller companies might not be able to afford a subscription, they might be able to attend the events and meet those who influence via this channel.

Remember way back in Chapter 2 when I mentioned seats on boards, some that you might pay for? This is a perfect venue for you to shape outcomes in your industry through a seemingly volunteer activity. When you sit on a relevant board or subcommittee of groups sponsoring industry content, you *shape* what gets discussed and how it's presented to large audiences. Ideally, you might even be the one to decide who gets to present the message—*you*.

4. Prime Communication for a Sub Prime

For companies in the supply chain of a large prime, you may feel you are one, two or three layers from the customer (agency or Congress) communications. Sometimes you can feel like a mushroom, living in the shadow of the big tree only occasionally receiving the light and water (funding and information), you need to grow.

- Does your Prime instruct you on the status of the program?

    - Or do you communicate relevant information "up" to your Prime?

    - If your prime does not instruct you on the status of the program, do you engage it to get the status?

- At what level of the Prime's organization do you interface routinely?

    - Is it limited to the supply chain and writer of the purchase order?

    - Do the leadership teams have any ongoing dialogue?

    - Are you limited to large gatherings of the other suppliers serving the prime?

    - Do you have an ongoing technical conversation with the prime?

- Do you even know which program your product supports?

o It's not uncommon for classified programs to have specific communications barriers.

- Fear of upsetting the Prime can needlessly limit good communication. Subs can sometimes be the first line of awareness to a problem for a Prime.

5. Prime Communciation

- Do you know what message the subs are sending?

- Do the subs know your script?

- Have you limited the messaging—either intentionally or unintentionally?

- What may not be important for you as the prime may be critical to the sub. Do you know the critical messages for your subs?

Ask Yourself:

If you wore the hat of a member of your customer constellation for a week or a month, what perception of your company would you come away with? That's what I'm getting at!

Means: The "How To"

Means are the action steps—the "how." They are the ongoing interactions that mirror solid and well-worn sales and business development actions. For example:

- Learning the federal customer culture by participating in events where face-to-face contact takes place: seminars, industry days, trade shows and lunch-and-learns.

- Taking advantage of opportunities for field visits where end users can give unvarnished feedback on the real need (read eventual requirement).

- Do you send or receive newsletters with content of mutual interest with federal customers or potential federal customers?

- Do you follow relevant groups on LinkedIn where your federal customer and competitors might also engage in dialogue? If so, do you participate by submitting or commenting on what's published?

- What sort of meeting rhythm have you established with your customer constellation? Does it have any relationship to the Fiscal Year of interest or the status of the budget request outlined in Chapter 6?

- Are those meetings scheduled with a sense of purpose or timing or did your CRM tool tell you it's time to send an email to touch base? Worse, did your CRM tools send something automatically that lacks personalization and looks like spam?

- Does your team know "the ask?" What does that mean? Read on.

Thinking back to the 3 rings, do you see when you coordinate and align your means and messaging throughout your customer constellation you become a ubiquitous figure? That is the goal. You need to be in all of these places.

Figure 21: The Ubiquitous You

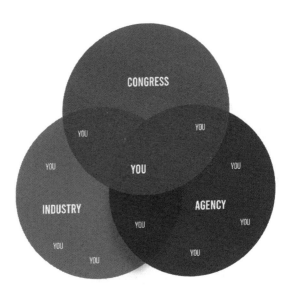

The Ask

Telling your story efficiently and effectively makes all the difference. Let's dig into this concept of "the ask."

Congress uses a tool that you can use to explain your message. It is called the Congressional White Paper. Insiders simply call it the white paper. But we're not talking about what you think of as a traditional white paper: a lengthy technical paper or a thesis with extensive supporting documentation and footnotes. A Congressional White Paper is your story told in one single sheet of paper. Remember the discussion about time back in Chapter 4? Specifically, that time is the critical element that runs through all Congressional activity? The White Paper is a highly effective tool that helps you tell a better story while being respectful of everyone's time.

A White Paper has four basic headings:

1. **Issue**—The problem to be solved, stated in 1-2 sentences at most.

2. **Background**—The "how we got here" story. Why the situation needs to be fixed.

3. **Discussion**—Supporting facts that lead the reader toward your proposed solution.

4. **Recommendation (The Ask)**—What must be done.

Telling your story with a single sheet of paper is much more difficult than it sounds. We are used to filling the air with words while we think out loud explaining our solution the government agency should adopt. We may think we can read a room and we're engaging with our customer. Often, doing so just burns up the clock and the customer is ready to move on.

Congressional staffs, with so much coming at them in a given day, must zealously manage their time. Condensing critical information to its essential elements allows them to move through thousands of issues quickly. While agencies might not necessarily demand the same brevity, the learning point can serve you and your team well.

Pro Tip:

Distilling your ask to the one-page White Paper forces you to be concise, saves everyone time in the discussion phase and gets you invited back for future meetings to participate in solutions.

Example:

I work with a relatively new software company, Beast Code. The CEO of Beast Code is an unassuming and unabashed techie. Beast Code does very complex things with relational databases that dramatically simplify training for the military end user. The capability has developed extremely quickly, far outpacing the speed with which the traditional budget process requests funding. These are the core elements of his white paper:

> **ISSUE**—Training can be delivered to Navy sailors at a fraction of the current cost.
>
> **BACKGROUND**—The Navy has spent hundreds of millions of dollars on schoolhouse training for each class of ship and type of aircraft.
>
> **DISCUSSION**—The Navy's training methods are not keeping up with what technology can now deliver into the sailor's hands. (Demonstrate a wow capability with a 2-minute demo)
>
> **RECOMMENDATION**—Congress helps the Navy jumpstart to a new level of high caliber sailor learning by applying $X dollars to X program.

Following the exact white paper formula of distilling a highly complex capability to its essence, the CEO earned praise from seasoned Congressional staff. He was regularly thanked by his audiences on the Hill for being "the best meeting of the day." His discipline in telling a tight story well in about 8 to12 minutes, with a reasonable "ask" that solved a real problem for the end user, garnered him millions of dollars in Congressional support. A finely tuned pitch can amp up your bottom line in a hurry.[5]

In government business, the difference between 5 percent growth and 30 percent growth in a year can be one opportunity.

Some say, "If you haven't written about it, you haven't thought about it." I agree with that mantra, but I'll take it a step further: If you can't get the story onto a single sheet of paper, it's not a tight enough story.

Influencing is not dissimilar from storytelling. A well-told story could translate to a favorable outcome. If you can do that, you will have real influence. A well-written story can help your many messengers and advocates speak from the same tightly worded script.

---

[5]For sample redacted, real-life white paper examples go to http://www.capitolintegration.com/3-ringcircus

PART III: Showtime!

Chapter 9: The Trapeze Act—It's All in the Timing

"Timing isn't the main thing,
it's the only thing."
—*Miles Davis*

A client of mine sells sophisticated ammunition used at the platoon level by soldiers in battle. One of its product lines is sold to non-NATO allies of the US. The approval process for foreign sales is formal, strict and sometimes purposely opaque. Uncertainty in approvals was creating uncertainty in the company's ability to meet financial targets. It didn't have the time or resources to devote to tracking this complex approval process through its many stages. Many individuals in the agency portion of the customer constellation don't have a meaningful appreciation of business pressures associated with profit and loss, or with being publicly traded.

The company came to me to help it gain better visibility on the status of approvals. I was able to demonstrate methods of sharing legitimate business concerns with the customer constellation. Specifically, we highlighted how lack of production schedule consistency directly impacted product costs to the government and allied customer. Understanding the mutual timetables helped the customer constellation and the client. Communication was improved, meaningful information was shared more openly and product costs and deliveries became more predictable. Timing matters throughout the rings of influence.

The Budget Timeline

The budget process follows a clear timeline, year after year. (See Figure 22). Exceptions always will occur, but there is a method to the madness. If you want the process to work to your advantage, you must learn it.

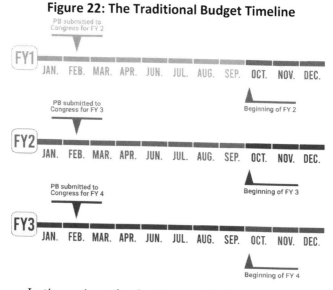

Figure 22: The Traditional Budget Timeline

Let's review the budget cycle briefly. The PB is produced for the coming fiscal year in advance, and is traditionally submitted to Congress on the first

Monday of February. The fiscal year runs from October 1st through September 30th. In Figure 22, the Fiscal Year 2 Budget is sent to Congress in February of Fiscal Year 1. Congress then considers and approves the budget via authorization and appropriations legislation. This process typically carries on throughout the summer. The House and Senate have until the end of September to pass a budget for the coming fiscal year.

You can see a pattern; there are at least 3 federal budgets in some stage of development or execution at any one time. Let's lay them out:

1. The budget being executed right now.

In Figure 22, this would be Fiscal Year 1. This budget is at its tail end. It has already gone through the full budget cycle and passed by Congress through an appropriations bill and signed into law. The budget funds have already been obligated within agencies. The money is in the government's checkbook, ready to be spent on contracting vehicles.

2. The budget for the immediate next fiscal year.

In Figure 22 this is Fiscal Year 2. This budget has been passed from the agencies, through OMB, and over to Congress. The House and Senate are marking it in the committees and subcommittees. Congress evaluates this budget for the coming fiscal year from roughly February through September 30th. The new fiscal year begins October 1st of each year.

3. The budget for the Fiscal Year two years into the future.

In Figure 22 this is Fiscal Year 3 in our hypothetical cycle. This budget is two years away from its execution and is still being prepared and reviewed within the agencies. It has not gone to OMB yet.

Be Ahead Of The Game

You should work the windows of opportunity well before the contract stage. If you are waiting for the RFP, you've missed years of opportunity to exercise influence within the 3 rings as the budget was developing.

Test Yourself:

At what point in the fiscal year have you taken these actions?

☐ Identify and cultivate champions in the 3 rings: Agency, Industry, Congress.

☐ Help your agency customer define what capability they need and to define the requirement.

- Coordinate across the many stakeholders in your area of interest.

- Connect with, listen to, share ideas and collaborate with agency contacts.

- Publish articles in trade journals, participate in industry panels where your issues were debated.

- Educate decision enablers, decision influencers, and decision makers in the 3 rings.

- Baked your solution into the RFP.

Seeing The Whole Picture

Spending that is carried out on contracts today is the result of budget decisions made as many as three years ago. The multiple budgets in motion represent near-, mid- and long-term opportunities for you to influence outcomes. The sooner you start shaping the process, the better chance you have of shifting the field in your favor. Beginning with the outcome in mind (Chapter 8), the various horizons of opportunity become more clear: near- (Fiscal Year 1), mid- (Fiscal Year 2), and long-term (Fiscal Year 3).

Figure 23: Moments of Opportunity by Fiscal Year

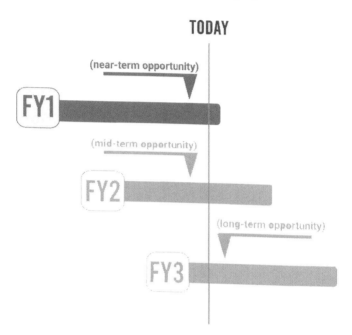

Figure 23 shows you the -near, -mid, and -long-term opportunities you have to influence the 3 budgets at play.

Right now, you are operating at the vertical line denoting "Today." This moment. Starting at today and moving to the right, you can gauge your relative positioning to the 3 budgets, moving along their own development timeline. This -year flow continues to repeat itself each year and becomes a perpetual cycle. In Figure 24 you'll note a fourth year added to demonstrate the possibility for even longer term research, planning, relationship building and positioning.

It is not complicated to grasp this recurring rhythm of budget cycles. Yet, many business leaders struggle to keep the various federal fiscal years straight in their conversations. Confusing the terms in front of your customers detracts from your credibility.

Don't surrender credibility. Demonstrate your command of the process.

Who Do You Call? When?

Notice, the closer you get to the budget execution year, when the contracts are awarded, the closer you are to running out of time. Meaning, it is much more difficult to influence the process the closer you get to the prime budget year you are targeting. Your engagement strategy requires thoughtful consideration of timing. Now that you understand the particular points in time when you should be shaping different budgets the questions become: Where do I direct my influence? Who do I contact when?

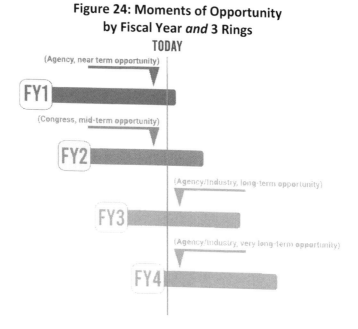

Figure 24: Moments of Opportunity by Fiscal Year *and* 3 Rings

Figure 24 begins to reveal where the 3 rings and the 3 budgets overlap. Recalling the 3 rings and the players in the customer constellation, you can layer your outreach to those individuals on top of the timelines for each fiscal year of interest. I have found that while all the individuals in your constellation matter, different people become relevant at different points in the process.

When looked at in the aggregate, the preferred times to connect become obvious.

For example, it doesn't make sense to approach industry contacts to form a partnership during FY1, an execution year. That budget is already formed and contracts are likely in place.

Similarly, it doesn't make sense to approach Congress soliciting support for the FY3 budget, because that budget is still in the long-term opportunity phase. You should focus your efforts on the agency and industry contacts in your constellation. The optimal way to approach Congress at this point would be to sell them on your issues for the FY2 budget. Looking at Figure 24, you can see that for FY2 you are in the mid-term opportunity zone. The PB for FY2 has been delivered to Congress. At this point, you know whether the Executive branch has prioritized your program because you have done your research and read the budget documents. **Remember when I said if it's not funded, it's not real? Well, *if it wasn't in the PB, it's not real.* Y**our only chance to intervene and get the funding you need is to lobby for support in Congress and convince them to mark the budget line that fell short in the PB. Engaging Congress for FY2 should be your top priority during this opportunity window.

Yes, It's a *Slow* Process

The budget process is a longer game than you might realize. That doesn't mean it's too hard or that you don't have the time or resources to commit for the long haul. As companies align their internal activities with the right windows of opportunity, the process becomes infinitely easier to shape. Now that you have a firm sense of how different budgets impact your business plan in different ways at different times, you can adjust your strategy accordingly. _It may be slow, but you cannot afford to get behind!_

In the next chapter, I'll bring all of the pieces of the puzzle together and show you how to maximize your efforts to achieve the best outcome.

Chapter 10:
You are the Ring Master

"Great things may come to those who wait, but only the things left by those who hustle."
—*Abraham Lincoln*

A small company, with fewer than 25 employees, came to me interested in end-of-fiscal-year sweep-up funds; federal dollars that would go unobligated if not put on an available contract. Many companies hear of the annual sweep-up drill, but have no idea how to position themselves. The company incorrectly thought the day-to-day agency contact had the authority to decide who gets the unobligated funds.

I was able to walk my client through the perpetual cycles of the fiscal years and how and when timing supported conversations at the right point in the customer constellation. I helped the company understand how the financial managers in DoD viewed their responsibilities to obligate funds in a measured way throughout the year. Together, we developed a near-term engagement plan focused on the execution year. Sweep up funds are as close to end game as can be, but the company that's prepared knows how to be positioned for the right conversation at the right time.

The salesperson or business that truly masters the 3-ring circus of federal sales has a deep understanding of how the customer constellation, a decision mapping methodology, funding and policy processes and budget timeline all come together to yield a successful sales outcome.

It's useful to maintain ongoing communications with contacts in each of the 3 rings. Keeping in mind which Fiscal Year they can affect and where they fall on the decision map will help you hone the most appropriate message at the right time. The messaging plan you create as a result should translate directly to your engagement strategy spreadsheet, allowing you to proceed in a methodical, intentional fashion. I promise you, this is the mode of engagement that will bring the best results.

Figure 25: Map of Influence

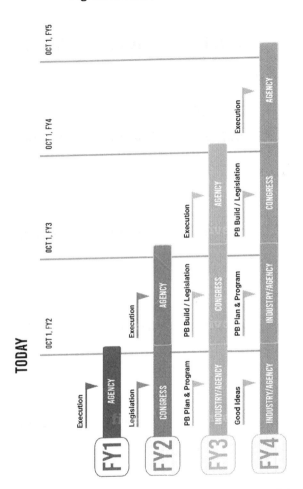

Let's outline which conversations you need to be having with your customers according to Fiscal Year.

FY1—Execution Year

In the execution year, you are primarily concerned with the status of your contract. It is possible that there might be some unobligated funds that did not go on contract for another project and are available to be diverted to you. These opportunities take the form of a reprogramming or an end-of-year sweep up. Maintaining contact with your agency counterpart can provide insight into the likelihood of capturing these extra funds. The government is famous for adhering to a use-it-or-lose-it mentality. They want to obligate every single dollar. Leftover funds will otherwise expire. Stay on the lookout and be in communication with your agency. In the execution year, focus on getting your funds on contract, ensuring your agency implements policy favorably, and maintaining your constellation of contacts.

FY2—Legislative Year

Congress is still evaluating your mid-term opportunities. If you are attempting to influence your agency for FY2 today, they won't help you and your contact will recognize you don't know the process. During the legislative year, focus on reacting to the PB when it comes out in February/March, influencing legislation as it's developed in Congress, keeping a pulse on the committee hearings and maintaining your agency contacts to keep them informed.

FY3—Plan and Program Year

Engaging industry and agency customers best influences your long-term opportunities. During the plan and program year, you are presenting conceptual ideas, imaginative solutions and coordinating within the industry.

FY4—Good Idea Year

While this seems a long way from the funding opportunity or policy outcome, this is the opportunity to have the maximum impact on positioning your product or policy idea. This is a good time to evaluate your position in your industry, consider board memberships, attend conferences and make yourself a part of the conversation. This is the time to focus on recognizing significant problems your company can address for the government and plant seeds for consideration of your solutions above others.

Putting the Puzzle Together

You've now gained an appreciation for process, messaging, influence and timing.

Let's flash back to Chapter 4 and review the "Who Decides" chart.

Figure 26: Decision Mapping

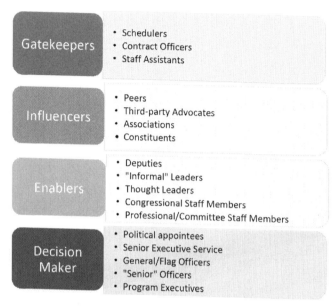

Now that you've thought about which rings you need to focus on for the different fiscal year plans, go back to your customer constellation and review which individuals you have in each of your rings. Write down their names, titles, organizations and contact information (which you may have gotten from a well-vetted subscription service). Input the information to your engagement strategy spreadsheet.

Now, looking at Figure 26, where do those specific individuals fall on the decision-mapping construct? Remember, one person can occupy multiple roles.

Check the cells accordingly in your spreadsheet: Gatekeeper, Influencer, Enabler, or Decision Maker. Everyone has a label? Good, next step.

Based on the ring of influence, the decision mapping label and the fiscal year you are targeting, what course of action do you need to take with each of these individuals?

Contacting a Decision Maker doesn't have to happen late in the process just because their role is to make the final decision. If you need a Decision Maker on your side for a FY3 budget item, start building that relationship now. Who is the Gatekeeper that leads to that Decision Maker? If you need to get to that Decision Maker a couple of years down the line, now might be the time to research the organization chart, find out who the Gatekeeper is, and contact them to set up a meeting. Or find out if the Decision Maker is speaking at any upcoming engagements and add them to your calendar so you can attend.

Plan Like a Pro

When you map your customer network, consider the 3 rings, and align your activities and engagements appropriately to the budget timeline, you begin to consider a much more efficient application of resources. You will also find you are able to influence high quality outcomes that might not otherwise have happened. A more time-oriented approach aligns your ideas and engagement activities with the budget process that remains in perpetual and relative motion.

So, how do you keep track of all these moving parts? Fiscal years, influencers, decision makers and contacts? It is a lot. No doubt about it. But that's why you create a plan. Here's another look at my engagement strategy model[6]:

Figure 27: The Engagement Plan – Part IV

ISSUE A (FY 3)	Title	Gatekeeper	Influencer	Enabler	Decision Maker	Message	Notes	Contact
Industry								
Bill Jones	VP, Supply Chain	X				We need to notify suppliers of 3-year forecast	Speaking at Industry Day	Bjones@ prime.com
Terry Smith	Contracting officer				X	We must be on contract by 1 May		
Agency								
Mr. Big	Asst Secretary				X	Foreign competition is a concern.		jking@ agency.gov
Mike Richards	Program Mgr		X	X		RFP must be issued by 31 Jan		mrichards@ agency.gov
Ms. King	Scheduler/EA	X	X				Don't call on Mondays	jking@ agency.gov
Congress								
Lisa Abernathy	HASC PSM		X	X	X	Need to coordinate with Rep Smith's team	Will take meeting before mark	first.last@ mail.house.gov
Roy Willow	Rep. Smith MLA	X				Need project sheet inputs by 15 Jan	Inputs due March 1st	first.last@ mail.house.gov

[6]For access to a template of Figure 27, go to http://www.capitolintegration.com/3-ringcircus .

Breaking it down by ring of influence and putting a contact plan in a matrix provides a handy visual for keeping track of the moving parts and their relative meaning. Whether you have 1 issue or 15 issues, breaking it down to the essential elements of an engagement plan can organize your efforts for maximum efficiency. At Capitol Integration, I track dozens of issues for each fiscal year using this exact methodology. You can too!

Figure 27 can be used in a printed format on a simple 5 by 8 card, projected onto a conference room screen when briefing your team or carried in a smart phone as drop box file. Figure 27 is highly simplified here, but can be tailored to the nth degree. It can have many, many columns and rows. The point is the columns and rows have purpose and relate directly to a time and place in the process. It's not simply a list of names and contacts, but an inherent focus.

You've identified who you need to see and when. You've thought about the message. You understand where you are in the process and to whom you are speaking, so the message has the best chance to be received and fairly evaluated. Having a tight message orchestrated over time, you'll be able to present to the customer constellation in a confident manner and know that you're in the right place at the right time.

Chapter 11: The Final Act

This book was written with the idea you could substantially improve your government sales if you had a more complete understanding of how federal sales opportunities evolve and where legitimate windows of influence exist. I reinforced the idea that companies of all sizes have the same opportunity to engage in the federal process. In this country, you have a right to participate—use it!

Let's review what you learned:

You identified the elements of the 3-Ring Circus and who impacts the decisions and support you need for your sale. You learned the critical details of the Main Acts in Part II. You now have a refined perspective on how to convey your critical information so that it makes sense. Lastly, you discerned the critical impact of timing in Part III.

Along the way, I highlighted some tips you can bring to immediate effect for your business. You completed various exercises to help you develop your personal playbook. Playbook exercises were introduced to get you moving in the right direction immediately. Visually appealing and easy-to-replicate tools were presented to assist you and your team in planning your own tailored approach. Lastly, specific definitions of terms within the process were clarified so you can communicate with confidence throughout your customer constellation.

Putting it all together, you've gained a better appreciation for the significance of timing, alignment and positioning in relation to a process that remains in perpetual motion.

Now it's back to you. I wish you continued success!

Encore: Resources from Gene Moran and Capitol Integration

- Full service government relations support to include lobbying and business development.

- Strategy development and implementation.

- Government sales team coaching.

- Tailored Seminars on the Federal Sales Process.

- Subscribe to Capitol Integration's *Quick Hits - What it Means* newsletter.

Learn more at http://www.capitolintegration.com

Acknowledgments

My wife, Julie, has been by my side my entire adult life. She is a constant source of love and support, without which none of my professional life would ever have been possible. Family separation was a necessary fact of life through nearly 25 years of service in the US Navy. As with all service families, that burden fell all too heavily on my family that remained at home. Julie miraculously kept the home fires burning and raised our four daughters into the wonderful young women they are today. Julie's never-ending love and dedication afforded me the luxury to pursue a subsequent corporate career and then launch our own business. I say it to all who listen, "we live in a great country," that affords such opportunities. Behind every opportunity I have ever enjoyed, was Julie.

Caroline Gelinne and I have worked together for several years with Capitol Integration. Caroline's gift of framing my concepts and examples into a coherent storyline has made this book much more readable than it otherwise might have been! Some say, "everyone has a book in them." I would add, "…if you have someone like Caroline to help you."

Dan Janal at PRLeads provided superb editing and ongoing guidance as this book came to life. Dan is far more than a developmental editor and marketing expert. He takes ownership in his work. The content was strengthened throughout the process and I believe it shows in this edition of *Pitching the Big Top: How to Master The 3-Ring Circus of Federal Sales.*

The book was made better and more readable with the support of editorial counsel provided by LtGen Greg Newbold, USMC (Ret), CAPT Terry O'Brien, USN (Ret) and Amy Showalter. Their collective feedback challenged me to try harder to get it right while keeping it simple.

Finally, thank you to Anna David and her team at Light Hustle Publishing!

Gene Moran
President, Capitol Integration
gene@capitolintegration.com
616-951-GOVT

Made in the
USA
Monee, IL

14641892R00104